"Wow. Jennifer Grant's *MOMumental: Adventu___* ___ *of Raising a Family* is more than a parenting boo__. __ __ __ a must-read for every mom (and dad!). With gut-wrenching honesty, Grant reminds us that imperfection should be celebrated, not feared, because we find beauty, grace, and redemption in the messiness of real life. A life-changing book that will inspire you to enjoy a calm, connected life with your children, no matter how imperfect."

Kirk Martin
founder of CelebrateCalm.com and CelebrateADHD.com

❖

"Readers have come to expect humor, warmth, and wisdom from Jennifer Grant. And *MOMumental* does not disappoint. Packed with stories of her successes and failures as a mom, Grant gives moms—and dads—a real treasure in this book: the knowledge that none of us is perfect, and yet each of us is up to the momumental task of building a great family."

Caryn Dahlstrand Rivadeneira
author of *Grumble Hallelujah* and *Mama's Got a Fake I.D.*

❖

"Jennifer Grant has done it again. *MOMumental*, marked by Grant's trademark humor, is a delicious weaving of her insights on parenting and family life. By just a few pages in, I was musing to myself, *Man, she's the real deal*. Though Grant humbly confesses her faults and foibles, it's crystal-clear to the rest of us that she's really got a good handle on this whole parenting business. Read this book. You'll be glad you did. I was."

Margot Starbuck
author of *Small Things with Great Love*,
The Girl in the Orange Dress, and *Unsqueezed*

❖

"Jennifer Grant's new book is as refreshing as a latte or wine break, as forgiving as your best friend, and a lot cheaper than a therapist. By sharing her hard-won personal wisdom and witty, intelligent writing, Grant will make you realize that your kids will be fine—and so will you. Though her personal faith infuses her philosophy, this book never seems preachy. She provides a great example for all parents trying to raise kids at a healthy distance from the most offensive aspects of popular so-called culture."

Meg Cox
author of *The Book of New Family Traditions:*
How to Create Great Rituals for Holidays & Everydays

❧

"*MOMumental* did two things I didn't believe any book could do: Its wit and wisdom so completely enraptured me, I found myself taking notes—both mental and with actual pen and paper—so that I could return to its vast treasure trove of practical and spiritual wisdom and share it with others. Moreover, it elicited such from-the-bottom-of-my-soul laughter and delight that I caused a full-blown scene on the cross-country plane ride where I read it. *MOMumental* is a book about parenting, family, and intentional relationships for readers who normally avoid such fare like an overzealous street evangelist. (Raises hand.) Through the marvelous honesty and infectious humor with which Jennifer recounts her parenting adventures—each of them grounded in deeply inviting and transparently authentic real-world faith—*MOMumental* is a delightful and surprising gift to us all, one that I already have begun pressing into the hands of anyone who crosses my path (beginning with my seatmates and the flight attendants on that ride from Washington, DC to California.) Fasten your seat belts, folks; you're in for an unforgettable ride. (Oh, and parents: Don't forget to put your own oxygen masks on *first* before helping those around you. Really.)"

Cathleen Falsani
award-winning journalist and author

❧

"After graduate studies in child development, I was certain of one thing: the only parenting book that I would ever consider giving to a friend would be Bettelheim's *A Good Enough Parent*. The title says it all. With Jennifer Grant's new book, *MOMumental*, I could feel confident passing along a companion text. Through her engaging stories, Grant lets us know how she journeyed from the dream of becoming an exceptional mother to her understanding that parenting is a messy and joyous art. Jennifer Grant does not give us prescriptions or answers. She shares the wisdom about parenting that she developed on this journey."

Jim Gill
musician, author, and child development specialist

✤

"Once again, Jennifer Grant has written a memoir about parenting and family life that makes you want to sneak into her house and magically become one of her children, for as long as you can get away with it. And not because she is 'the perfect mother,' but because she is both candid about her struggles as a mom and yet also inspiring with her dreams and ideals for her family. Grant reminds us that amidst all the craziness and stress of modern-day parenting—no matter how flawed our mothering may sometimes be—we are all more than capable of doing that which is most important for our kids: loving them, connecting with them, being smitten with them. And I know that after you read *MOMumental*, you'll be smitten with Grant and her wonderful book."

Helen Lee
author of *The Missional Mom*

✤

"This lovely, honest look at mothering will encourage every woman who has wondered if she has what it takes to succeed at life's most important calling. Filled with humor, poignant anecdotes, and great advice, *MOMumental* should be on every mom's shelf."

Dale Hanson Bourke
author of *Everyday Miracles* and *Embracing Your Second Calling*

✤

"Like a much-needed, laughter-filled conversation with the best of friends, reading *MOMumental* centers me as a mom, reminding me to be content with the blessings of sometimes-messy family life. And it inspires me to ask myself the right questions, to seek after what's truly meaningful, and to dream the very best dreams for my kids."

Kelli B. Trujillo
author of *Faith-Filled Moments: Helping Kids See God in Everyday Life* and *The Busy Mom's Guide to Spiritual Survival*

✣

"In *MOMumental*, Jennifer Grant stares down the monster of idealized parenthood, laying bare her own dreams and failures as a mom and ultimately offering up a gentler, more effective model. Any mom living the competitive lifestyle that is modern motherhood will find relief, companionship, and encouragement in this delightful book."

Lara Krupicka
writer, speaker, and mother

✣

"*MOMumental* is like having a cup of tea with a wise sister. Affirming, funny, and poignant, Jennifer Grant gives us all permission to loosen up, make mistakes, and love our kids like crazy."

Monica Selby
freelance writer, blogger, and mommy of three

✣

"I love Jennifer Grant. In fact, every mom deserves at least one Jen Grant in her life. She's that friend who offers a healthy perspective, a good laugh, and a good cry—sometimes all at the same time—while she affirms, honors, and celebrates you and your life as a mom. Grant specializes in joy. And her new book is an intelligent, honest, and life-affirming memoir celebrating the unparalleled joys, unending rewards, and monumental challenges of motherhood—the good, the bad, and the wacky making. You will love *MOMumental*!"

Amy Hilbrich Davis
mom of seven, CEO of FamilyLife Success, parent and family engagement expert, creator of the balance MAP

MOMUMENTAL

Adventures in the Messy Art of Raising a Family

Jennifer Grant

WORTHY
PUBLISHING

Published by Worthy Publishing, a division of Worthy Media, Inc., 134 Franklin Road, Suite 200, Brentwood, Tennessee 37027.

HELPING PEOPLE EXPERIENCE THE HEART OF GOD

eBook available at www.worthypublishing.com

Audio distributed through Oasis Audio; visit www.oasisaudio.com

Library of Congress Control Number: 2012934734

Published in association with the literary and marketing firm of C. Grant & Company, Wheaton, IL.

For foreign and subsidiary rights, contact Riggins International Rights Services, Inc.; www.rigginsrights.com

ISBN: 978-1-617950-74-2 (trade paper)

Cover Design and Photography: Grey Matter Group
Interior Design and Typesetting: Kimberly Sagmiller, FudgeCreative

Printed in the United States of America
12 13 14 15 16 17 18 SBI 10 9 8 7 6 5 4 3 2 1

For my family—
David, Theo, Ian, Isabel, and Mia—
with love,
gratitude,
and big, fledgy yesses.

CONTENTS

No doubt about it: children are a gift from the LORD.
—**Psalm 127:3** CEB

*It is easier to build strong children
than to repair broken men.*
—**Frederick Douglass**

*Knowing that we can be loved exactly as we are
gives us all the best opportunity for growing into
the healthiest of people.*
—**Fred Rogers**

INTRODUCTION

Velveteen Parenting
Adventures in Becoming Real

I always wanted to be a mother.

Scratch that. Let me begin again.

I always wanted to be a *very good mother*—exceptional even.

I pictured myself with a happy houseful of children. We would play games together: kickball, Monopoly, charades. We'd have tea parties and sleepovers and go on epic family vacations we would remember and talk about for the rest of our lives. The Galápagos Islands. Paris. The Great Wall of China. I would appreciate the children, never sighing or moaning about how much work it was or how much it cost to raise them.

And, like you I'm sure, I was intent to bring only what was most positive about my childhood into my own parenting. When we actually become parents, however, we find that the disappointment, sleep deprivation, and the basic demands of—you know—being *adults* tug at the neat seams of our resolve until we find ourselves saying things to our kids that we swore we'd never say. We do the things we promised we'd never do. Caught in a moment of "Go clean your room!" or "How many times have I told you . . ." we hold our heads in our hands like that iconic Munch painting, *The Scream*, and shriek, "That's it! I've officially turned into my mother!" (At that point, either we laugh at ourselves and realize there's nothing wrong with that, or we pick up the phone and call a therapist. Both are perfectly reasonable responses.)

When I was growing up, I wondered whether my parents' divorce prohibited me from eventually creating a marriage that would last. Did a person have to soak up—minute by minute and day by day—the stellar examples of parents in order to create a solid marriage and family as an adult? I would hear myself referred to as a "child of a broken home" as though a damaged building—not two human beings— had somehow brought me into the world. When I heard the phrase, shame washed over me, and I wondered whether tattered relationships were my destiny.

In the years leading up to my parents' divorce, woundedness pulsed through my house at uneven intervals, filling the air with a kind of stale emotional odor, like when the heating system is turned on after a long summer. The vents blow dust and a musty smell through the house, affecting each room.

Everything seemed to be falling apart at home. And according to the evening news, it was no better in the world at large. President Nixon had resigned. Scientists were making babies in test tubes. The mass suicide in Jonestown. Patty Hearst. An oil crisis.

My religious faith confused me too. At church, my least favorite verses in the Bible often loomed over me like dark clouds. The sins of the fathers, the pastors said, would be visited on the children. Not *might be*, but *would be* visited on the sinner's offspring. Every time I heard those verses, I felt jinxed. I certainly didn't want anybody's sins to "visit on" me. Not those of the father I barely knew or of the grandparents I'd never met. I wanted a strong marriage and a big, happy family someday.

(Curse-free, if you please.)

I used to wonder whether other people's families knew something mine didn't. I spied from the bushes as the magician who lived across the street worked with his mourning doves in his garage. I peered into family rooms as neighbors reclined in their La-Z-Boys in front of *Love Boat* and *Fantasy Island*. I strained to overhear adult conversations at friends' houses while we sat cross-legged on the floor playing with stuffed animals.

When I discovered Louise Fitzhugh's novel *Harriet the Spy*, I felt like I had found a soul mate. Harriet was quirky and curious, and she paid attention to the ordinary details of other people's lives. So I began to write my observations about people in black-and-white composition notebooks the way Harriet did.

Alice's mother keeps a drawer of candy bars in her kitchen. Alice and her brother David don't have to ask before taking one and they never have to eat health food like wheat germ or Tiger's Milk.

No one is allowed in Kim's living room and the carpet is vacuumed into straight lines. Kim's mother always dresses nicely, her hair is always done, and she always seems to be standing silently in front of a shiny kitchen sink.

Megan's parents keep to themselves. Their bedroom is on its own side of the house down a long, shadowy hall. It doesn't seem to bother anyone that the house is messy or that the doors stand open.

Every time I walk by, the front yard of Brandon's

house is filled with kids running around. Of the eight of them, some were adopted, some not. Some are white, some not. They like one another.

My parents divorced by the time I was in junior high school. It was around then that I heard myself referred to as a "latchkey kid." Yes, I had a key on a string around my neck or sometimes waiting for me under the front doormat. And yes, with a mother who had returned to school for her doctorate, I let myself into a quiet house after school every day.

But did I really need *another* maudlin nickname?

As a "latchkey kid from a broken home," my family fantasies continued. Sometimes when I pictured myself grown up and a mother, I could almost see the adult version of me (as played by, perhaps, *Hart to Hart*'s Stefanie Powers) pulling the door open wide for my kids and meeting them after school with a plate of just-out-of-the-oven Toll House chocolate-chip cookies and glasses of milk. Like the fictional Jennifer Hart, maybe I'd be a journalist with a secret life as a private investigator.

When my Jennifer-Hart-adult-self met the children at the door, the aforementioned cookies would be baked with *real chocolate chips* and accompanied by *store-bought milk*. This was imperative. The chocolate chips in my house at that time were generic and "chocolate-flavored" and seemed brushed with some kind of purplish wax. The grocery store had a whole aisle of generic products, bearing only the most basic descriptions of what was inside the packages. The lone design on the boxes or cans was a dreary olive green line and black stenciled letters: FLOUR. COLA. BAKING CHIPS. TUNA.

The milk we drank at home was made from a mix that was kept in a giant paper bag next to the water softener in the basement. After a trip to the grocery store with my mom, I'd lug a block of salt down into the basement and drop it into the softener, stepping back to avoid getting splashed, the muscles in my arms stretched long after walking the salt down two flights of stairs from the garage.

"Get some milk while you're down there, okay?" my mom would call from the kitchen, and I'd dip a glass measuring cup into the bag of powder to take up for that night's dinner.

We weren't poor, and we weren't rich. We had a house in a nice neighborhood in one of the most affluent counties in America. The schools were great, there was food on the table, and we had the clothes, books, and toys we needed. But things were very tight.

After my parents' divorce, my father moved to Texas and I didn't see him again until I was in college. "Our father, who art in Texas," my siblings sometimes joked. Back then, Texas was a sanctuary for what some referred to as "deadbeat dads." Texas provided men a safe haven from alimony and child support payments. Maybe these fathers had other reasons for relocating there. Perhaps they were infatuated with the Lone Star State or with cowboys and mechanical bulls. Later, though, it did seem it was likely more than a coincidence that *all* the men I heard of from our town who had left their families had moved to that same state so far away from our hometown in Illinois. I pictured them sitting together at a saloon, raising their glasses as the wooden doors swung open to reveal another father on the run from his family up north.

Saddled with bills (pun intended) and raising us while going to graduate school, my mother got the bags of powdered milk and other food and household items from a missionary organization in the town just north of where we lived. A child of the Depression, my mom knows how to stretch a dollar and is more interested in the life of the mind than in measuring up to the mythical Joneses. She is much more likely to notice a title on a bookshelf than someone's new kitchen cabinets.

My brother Drew still favors the strawberry Suave, the shampoo of our youth, brought home in bulk from the warehouse along with the milk powder. Four years older than I am, and more my playmate than our older siblings, Drew valiantly drank my milk most days after first creating a diversion to distract our mother.

When I attempted to sip the milk, I would gag. "I can't!" I would whine. "I'm going to throw up."

But we had to drink our milk—strong bones and teeth and all that.

My heroic brother took pity on me and came to my rescue every evening by pointing animatedly out the window at the backyard and shouting, "Oh, look! A rabbit!" or "What kind of bird is that?" Our mother would turn to the window, and while her back was to us, he'd exchange our glasses—his empty, mine full of the lumpy, ivory-colored liquid.

"Oh, I must have missed it," my mother would say, disappointed. "What color were its feathers?"

I realize that it wasn't very nice of us to exploit her gullibility. But you know what they say: desperate times call for desperate measures. Drew could be in prison right now for committing a heinous crime and I'd still think he was a saint for drinking glass after glass of that lukewarm powdered milk when we were kids. Even with ice cubes, it was nasty. I knew one thing for sure: when I grew up, my kids would have store-bought milk.

Cold, tasty, and white.

No stirring necessary.

The vision of my eventual family life came into even clearer focus when I worked as a babysitter in high school and college. I noted, with an anthropologist's vigilant and detached gaze, frazzled parents barking at their children before leaving me in charge and then, hours later when they were off having dinner at the country club, the children speaking in those same cutting tones with each other. I saw looks of cold hostility pass between the mothers and fathers of some of the children for whom I babysat. It strengthened my resolve. Such unpleasantness would *not* befall my home when I had children of my own.

There was no need for it. I would be in love with my husband, and he with me. I would model tolerance, good humor, and gentleness for my children, and they would mirror these traits.

I would be like a stone dropped into a pond, my children the ripples, spreading peace and goodwill as they echoed away from me into their own lives. Perhaps, I allowed, they might bicker on *extremely* rare occasions, but only when they were overtired or coming down with the flu. But at those jangly times, I would sashay into the room and know just what to say to calm them and help them reconnect, and they all would be back on track again. I wouldn't spank them, shame them, or even raise my voice toward them. I wouldn't need to—we would be in such sync with one another.

I also wouldn't be imprisoned by convention. As a result, my children would always be fully, joyfully, authentically themselves. I'd let them paint murals on their bedroom walls. I'd allow them to have a dozen different kinds of pets. (*You want a Saint Bernard? Of course! An iguana? Why not? A long-haired Persian cat? How exquisite!*) They'd choose their clothes and how they wanted to wear their hair.

Our home would be an oasis in an uncertain world.

I would break that old "sins of the fathers" curse and would not be burdened by childhood wounds.

I'd blow my sad memories into the wind, like dandelion seeds.

In my early thirties, as the mother of three young children, my Harriet-the-Spy-self remained hyper vigilant, ever on the lookout for examples of happy homes to emulate. While stationed for several hours a day on the sofa with a nursing baby and a clear view of the street, I watched a red van pull in and out of the driveway opposite my own. Six, eight, ten, twelve times a day, I saw my neighbor maneuver her van up the hill, into the garage, and then out again. The garage door went up, the red van pulled in or out, the door went down.

Where could she be going? I'd wonder, captivated.

Its driver, my across-the-street neighbor, was efficient, cheerful, and always in motion. Her dress was casual but pulled together, sort of like an L.L. Bean catalog model. Her children were attractive, polite kids who seemed to be decades older than my own. (Hers were—gasp!—already *all* in school.) As my baby napped, my neighbor's kids clambered around on their play set and threw a baseball in the yard with their father. They were in the gifted program at school and followed their mother's lead to be environmentally conscious and helpful toward those in need in the community.

I picked at the frayed fabric of my sweatpants, and I swooned.

At the time, I was a part-time reporter for a local newspaper and, enamored with my neighbor, I asked her whether she would agree to be interviewed for a feature story on what it meant to be a mother in the year 2000. Gamely, she agreed. I'd been spying on her for months, noting whatever details of her life I could glean from a distance; but for the story, she gave me access to her house, her schedule, and even the holy of holies, you might say—her massive, wood-paneled refrigerator.

I sat on the edge of my kids' green turtle sandbox in the backyard, writing the story as my children played nearby. My feet were buried and unburied by my toddler son Ian as I scratched away on a yellow legal pad with a marker that likely was a prize in a goody bag or a stumpy pencil taken from the pews at my church. I had long since abandoned my Harriet-the-Spy composition books as well as the pretentious fountain pens and Moleskine journals of my young adulthood.

But here I was, finally a professional journalist, writing from my suburban backyard. If Louisa May Alcott could write her novels with children running around the drawing room, certainly I could write features for the local paper with my bare feet submerged in cool sand.

I nervously awaited the publication of the profile on my neighbor, hoping she would approve of it. But I had nothing to fear—what was published in the paper was a sort of song of praise to the stay-at-home mother and to my neighbor in particular. The headline read "The Right Kind of Busy."

The week's groceries are unloaded into the refrigerator. Eight plastic jugs of milk form ranks. On the bottom shelf, twenty containers of yogurt stand at the ready. In the large pullout freezer drawer below, frozen meat and pizzas await. The only aberration from orderly rows and columns is a bowl of half-eaten ice cream, topped with chocolate syrup, a spoon stuck in it like an explorer's flag.

This kitchen, like so many kitchens belonging to school-aged children and their parents, is clearly the family's headquarters. Each person's schedule is noted on the calendar; everyone is assigned a color. Yet, in this meticulous environment, signs—including the ice cream sculpture in the freezer—reveal that real children live a real life here. . . .

Keeping kids in clean soccer uniforms, overseeing their academic progress, volunteering at their schools, delivering them to practice fields, and feeding them in the scant moments between work and school can take a Herculean effort from parents. Knowing that it is a choice—rooted in love for the child—to invest in one's children and their activities seems to help parents remain dedicated and armed with a sense of humor about the demands of their schedules.

And on it went, detailing my neighbor's good sense as well as the ways she was creating a balanced, happy home for her children. In this one person, this one seemingly ordinary neighbor, I'd finally found what I'd been seeking for so many years: the perfect mother making the perfect family.

I wanted to *be* her.

Not surprisingly, for the few years we lived across the street from each other, she was my parenting guru. I asked her advice on everything from treating a child's rash to whether to register my kids for an activity through the park district. I was always running across the road to chat with her as she pulled weeds or started on a walk with her dog. She was infinitely patient with me.

"Be there when they get out of school," she advised. "Then you get the real story of what happened that day before it all goes out of their minds."

Check.

"Pediatricians don't always trust you. They forget that moms spend every waking moment with their kids. You have to insist that you get in for an appointment when you know something's going on."

Got it.

When I confessed to her that I was trying to follow very closely in her footsteps, my neighbor laughed and tried to dissuade me from doing so. She confessed her mistakes to me, told me about the appointments or celebrations she had forgotten, and detailed how she sometimes felt confounded by the needs and personalities of her four children.

I chalked up such admissions to her modesty. My neighbor's house and children seemed perfect to me. She was involved at her church, a committed gardener, and always reaching out to the older people on our block. She was even her sons' Boy Scout den leader. In my mind, she was an ideal mother and had family life "down pat," whatever that expression meant. She made it all look so easy. You see, back then I was a believer in what author Carla Barnhill calls the "myth of the perfect mother."[1] Nothing she could say or do dissuaded me from seeing her in this rosy light.

One afternoon, I sat with my four children and her daughter, who was then around ten years old, in my front yard. The ice cream truck had made its way up our street, and in a fit of maternal zeal, I waved it down and bought treats for all the kids within sight. As my (perfect) neighbor's daughter ate her ice cream, she remarked that her brother—then in high school—was in trouble. *Big trouble.* I don't remember whether he had missed his curfew or had done poorly on a test, but whatever it was, she said it was a *very big deal.*

"Oh. Teenagers do stuff like that sometimes, don't they?" I said sagely, as though I had any clue what teenagers did and didn't do. At the time, I couldn't imagine my own kids as teens, arriving home late, or being asked to study for tests more academically rigorous than that of reciting the alphabet or tying their shoelaces.

"My mom was so mad she chased him up the stairs with a wooden spoon," the girl announced as she and the other kids jumped up from the grass to play.

A wooden spoon? I had no idea she has such a flair for the dramatic, I thought. *I bet* that *got his attention, the rascal!* I was awash in appreciation for my neighbor's good humor.

Later my neighbor told me about the incident and described the white-hot rage she had felt when she ran after her son. (*Rage? But I thought you were just being silly and theatrical!*) As she confessed her anger, I couldn't believe that she had been brought to such a point with her son. *How could* one's own child *be that infuriating?* Rage was chaotic and uncontrolled; it made me nervous. Committed as I was to keeping my fantasy alive, I quickly dismissed the idea that she could have experienced such a strong emotion.

Anomaly, I thought with a shrug, and then I complimented her on the lilies in her garden.

I'm sure she could have used a kind word at that moment and would have liked to be seen and accepted as the real-life person she was. But I had shaped her into something else. I had slapped a big label on her that read "Perfect Mom" and the letters were so shiny and appealing, I couldn't see past them to the real person standing in front of me.

Now, years later, after being broken in by time and exasperation and days when I want to run after my own kids with a wooden spoon, I no longer look to others or to myself to be ideal mothers. Now, like the Velveteen Rabbit, I've become, well, more *Real*. My fur's been rubbed off. My heart has stretched and expanded. The shine is gone. Now I can say with confidence that much as we may long to do so, we cannot create perfect homes and families. No matter how spiritually deep, deliberate, or disciplined we aspire to be, we can't completely escape the unpleasant parts of ourselves. We can't gather up all of our childhood memories, injuries, and longings like a heap of dirty laundry and load them into the washing machine to make every wrinkle and stain disappear. Whatever you call it—original sin, human nature, or just life—a vein of brokenness runs through every one of us. We must acknowledge the darker parts of ourselves, confess our mistakes and bad choices, accept forgiveness, and give ourselves the chance to start again. Over and over and over again.

These days, instead of focusing on creating a conflict-free home, raising picture-perfect kids, and being an ideal mother—comprised of equal parts June Cleaver, Eleanor Roosevelt, and Angelina Jolie—I have embraced a more realistic view of what I can and cannot do as a parent. This reality-based "Velveteen parenting" includes, but is not limited to, the following general guidelines:

- I choose my battles. Although I don't like it when my kids draw on their hands, chew the erasers off of their pencils, or overuse the word *like*, I try to overlook these misdemeanors.
- I know it's not even worth trying to puzzle out what is "the right kind of busy."
- I keep my eyes open and look with a critical—and often delighted—eye at what my culture is dishing up to my children and me. I try to teach my kids to

do the same and to appreciate that which is true and good.

- I remind myself that children are not little adults but are uniquely suited to grow, learn, and enjoy life in ways that many of us adults don't remember how to do anymore.

- I ask questions such as, *What do I want our family to be like? What are our individual gifts and perspectives? What connects us as a family and brings us joy?*

- I make certain things priorities in our family life— that we treat each other with respect as much as possible, that we eat together whenever possible, and that we attend church together as much as we can.

And I'm not ashamed that everyone from my kids' teachers to my friends to the children themselves knows how smitten I am with them. That I'm besotted and madly head-over-heels in love with my children underlies all of the precepts above, and I hope as they grow up and go out into the world, that big love will be a protection to them. I also pray that the way they have experienced love from my husband and me in their childhoods will affect the way they experience the reality of God's love throughout their lives.

If you picked up this book in hopes of reading a parenting manual with a definitive solution to the very best way to raise children, I'm afraid you'll be let down. In these pages, I don't advocate that you become a Tiger Mother, BFF Mom, Helicopter Mom, or Earth Mama to your kids. I don't know the best way to potty-train a toddler, to get children to prefer broccoli over caramel corn, or to ensure that teenagers don't engage in risky behavior such as driving too fast or sassing their parents. I don't know how to make the middle school years or algebra homework as rewarding to children as an afternoon at the beach. What I do know is that family matters and it is a constant source of joy, grace, and, yes, moments of real exasperation in my life.

This book, then, is just stories about family life and how I've come to appreciate the mess of it. I am grateful for my own happy, idiosyncratic, and imperfect family and the culture we are creating together.

I'm doing my best to raise strong children, not broken adults.

I wish all of this for you too.

CHAPTER 1

Fledge Words and Fairy Dust
Adventures in Saying Yes

A woman I admire once told me her parenting philosophy. Although my oldest child was only three at the time, I filed her words away in my mind and knew someday I'd return to them. The way I understood it, she and her husband began raising kids with a high proportion of "no"s, but increased the "yes"es each year. She said the job of parenting entailed letting out the rope, giving kids more freedom and room to roam as they grew.

She kept very close to her children when they were babies and toddlers. She had high standards for their behavior as they moved through school. Little by little, however, she and her husband made setting expectations a family affair, and their children were given more autonomy. By the time they were in high school, her children were independent and almost completely responsible for the consequences of their choices. The parents still had authority over the children and there were well-established household rules, but increasingly my friend and her husband allowed their kids to take risks, to make their own goals and decisions, and to set the course for their lives.

Po Bronson, child development expert and coauthor with Ashley Merryman of *Nurture Shock*, would likely nod at this approach to parenting. In his article "How Not to Helicopter" he writes, "Teens need opportunities to take good risks. . . . They need part of their life to feel real, not just a dress rehearsal for college. They will mature more quickly if these elements are in their life."[1]

Now my friend's three children are adults and, from what I have observed, they are connected, vital, and healthy people. They seem to enjoy their parents. They all graduated from college, and two are happily married.

I like the idea that as kids grow in wisdom and maturity, they will hear "yes" more often.

I have turned my wise friend's words over in my mind countless times over the years, visualizing myself literally releasing a skein of rope, foot by foot, as my children grow older. Now that my oldest child is in high school, I give him ample room to make his own decisions and to live with the consequences. I bite my tongue during finals week when he says he needs a break from studying and wants to go out with friends. I no longer keep close track of whether he's practicing his cello or how he's spending his money. I don't insist that he goes to summer camp or on church mission trips. I don't slip into his room when he's showering after a soccer game and drop his dirty uniform down the chute so it will be ready for the next game or tuck laundered gym clothes into his backpack. These things are his responsibilities now. If he goes to school having left an English paper in the printer or to soccer practice without his cleats, he'll be the one affected.

There are house rules he must follow and he knows his parents' values and expectations, but most of the decisions in his life are his to make. When he asks, we talk at length about what his father and I see as benefits or potential pitfalls of saying yes or no in a certain situation, but—the vast majority of the time—we leave decisions to him. In having the opportunity to make real decisions, my son matures and gains independence, and I catch glimpses of the adult he is becoming.

Yes.

James Joyce's striking novel *Ulysses* ends with it. That last unpunctuated chapter begins with the word *and* it abundantly appears throughout Molly's soliloquy. The book ends with her recollection of her husband Bloom's proposal: "and his heart was going like mad and yes I said yes I will Yes." After forty-some pages without the sentence ending, that final, capitalized "Yes" and the period that follows it make you catch your breath.

Yes.

E.E. Cummings' exceedingly punctuated work frolicked with it. He begins one poem with the words "yes is a pleasant country." The first stanza of another of his poems, "i thank You God for most this amazing," reads

> *i thank You God for most this amazing*
> *day:for the leaping greenly spirits of trees*
> *and a blue true dream of sky; and for everything*
> *which is natural which is infinite which is yes*[2]

Yes declares, "Of course! So be it!" It is a fundamental word for all sorts of creation. Friendships, marriages, transformations, treaties, inventions, art. Even saying the word *yes* guides our mouths into the shaping of a smile.

Yes, as my wonderful college English professor and priest, the late Reverend Dr. Joseph McClatchy said, is a "fledge word." Fledge words, he said, reach up toward heaven, seemingly taking wing to the Most High. The upward reaching of the letter Y, Father McClatchy pointed out, makes our spirits rejoice and stretch toward God.

The usual definition of the word *fledge* is to be capable of, or to have the feathers required, for flying. When a bird is "fledged," it can take flight. Fledge words reach up toward heaven, causing our hearts to soar when we speak them.

(*Yes*, Father McClatchy was delightfully eccentric.)

When my husband and I were engaged, almost twenty-five years ago, we hurried to Father McClatchy's office high in an old gothic building on our college campus that once was a stop on the Underground Railroad. Because he was a favorite professor and a priest at our church, David and I wanted him to be one of the first people to know of our engagement.

We knocked at the door.

"Yes? Come in! Come in!" Father McClatchy called.

I like to think that we were both pet students of his, but to be honest, I believe David was his real favorite. After all, it was David who more than once received grades of A++++ on his English papers. (Until I saw my boyfriend's grades, I was buoyed with pride when I received the occasional A+. I forgave David and decided to marry him anyway, the show-off.)

"Father," David began on that December afternoon, "there's something we want to share with you."

"Wait! Wait! Don't say a word!" Father McClatchy shouted, anticipating our news. "Not another word!"

A trim and spritely man with a neat beard and glasses, he jumped up from his desk, jogged around it, and busied himself at his stereo console. He chose an album and slipped it from its cardboard sleeve. (Remember record albums?) He then carefully set it on the turntable, lowered the needle, and as the music began, said, "Okay. Now. I want you to be *waltzing* when you say it."

As the music of Johann Strauss—I don't remember which piece but something along the lines of "The Blue Danube" or *Die Fledermaus*—filled the room, David and I did our best impression of a waltz and Father McClatchy sat on the edge of his desk and clapped his hands excitedly.

"*Now* tell me!" he shouted over the music.

"Father McClatchy!" David yelled. "We're engaged!"

"Hallelujah!" our professor cried. He shaped his arms goalpost style to suggest a capital *H* before wrapping us in his embrace. "Hallelujah! H! Fledge letter! Fledge word!"

What a superb way to begin a life together.

Yes. It *is* a pleasant country.

But then there's *no*. No is the lines in your datebook, the hands of the clock, the entries in your check register. No is a door closing, a disapproving shake of the head, a frown. Of course, No's not all bad. Not at all. No keeps us from hurting ourselves, No protects us, and No draws boundaries around cherished parts of our lives. It's not a fledge word, however. That's for sure.

When my eldest child was an infant, I heard Harvard child psychiatrist Robert Coles interviewed on the radio. He said that parents should start saying no to children at about nine months old. No saves them from running into the road and being hit by a car, putting their fingers in electrical outlets, or thinking it's acceptable to yank on the dog's tail.

No, Coles explained, gives children a message that bolsters their independence and self-esteem. It lets them know that someone more capable and bigger than they are is looking out for them. They want and need that sense of protection—desperately.

Isn't that why kids test our resolve and resist our authority?

"Are you in charge? Are you?" they ask. "Because believe it or not, I'm not really sure what I'm doing most of the time."

Well, as you know, they never ever actually come out and say that. They whine and cry and shout "Mine!" or "Everyone's allowed to go except me!" or "You're so unfair!" But, as Coles pointed out, children need the loving protection of their parents' No. I took Coles' words to heart and, from very young ages, my children have heard the word often.

But No can be damaging too.

Weeks after we waltzed in our English professor's office, David received a very different response to our engagement in the form of a letter sent through the campus mail.

"You're not going to believe this," he said, flipping the envelope onto my lap. We were sitting in the lobby of my dorm and, as he began paging through a magazine, I opened the letter. It was written by a woman my husband had known when he was growing up, another professor at the college. She implored him to call off our wedding plans.

My eyes stung as they grazed over her words: "dysfunctional family," "too special for her," "no chance for a successful marriage." Reading it, childhood fears about my inability to have a happy, stable marriage and family as an adult flew at me. It was the "sins of the fathers" argument, hurled at me in tidy cursive. I handed the letter back to David. He crumpled it and tossed it into the metal trashcan beside him.

"Go figure, right?" he said, before noticing my tears. "What? You're not going to take that seriously, are you?"

I was silent.

"It's just lies," he said, unperturbed.

Since that day, I've come to know the tone with which he spoke those words. David has a grudge-free and measured response to people he deems unreasonable—he shrugs them off. (I still have my learner's permit in this practice, and too often the Nos of my critics swirl around in my mind, knocking me off-balance.)

"Jen, she doesn't even know you. Or who we are together," David said. "Now forget it, and let's go get dinner."

At our wedding a few months later, with my bridesmaids wearing floral Laura Ashley dresses and my veil attached to a pink rose headband I nicknamed "The Hedge," Father McClatchy stood with David and me at the front of the church to join our lives together. In the service, a dear friend read "the love chapter" from the Bible. "Love suffers long and is kind; love does not envy; love does not parade itself, is not puffed up; does not behave rudely, does not seek its own, is not provoked, thinks no evil; does not rejoice in iniquity, but rejoices in the truth; bears all things, believes all things, hopes all things, endures all things" (1 Corinthians 13:4–7). I don't care how predictable it may be to read that passage at weddings; I think it's an excellent way to send two people into marriage. The couple hearing those words, as was true for David and me, will likely have no idea of how excruciatingly difficult it will be to be patient, to be kind, and, yes, even to *endure* each other through certain parts of life. But starting a marriage together cloaked in those words seems a strong protection, and even a sort of road map, for the journey ahead.

As David and I retreated down the aisle after being proclaimed husband and wife, two of our friends who had served as ushers in the wedding stood up in the balcony above us, removed their tuxedo jackets and turned around. On the back of their shirts, written in black electrical tape, was the word *YES*.

A quarter century after saying those big, fledgy yesses to each other on our wedding day, David and I continue to say yes to each other. Since they came into our lives, we love, endure, and believe in our children too, saying yes to them when we can. Ours has been as happy a marriage as any I know, by which I mean we have struggled through parched, desert places, enjoyed stunning moments of joy, and have learned over time to be loving partners to each other. Sometimes I experience an almost adolescent crush on him. (Have his eyes always been so blue? And those strong features? He brings Christopher Plummer's Captain von Trapp to mind, minus the whistle and cranky demeanor. But still . . . aye, aye Captain!) He looks over at me at those moments and I feel myself blush. Other days, the way he butters his toast so meticulously makes me want to scream. And why does he have to smash the garbage down in the kitchen trashcan so hard that the next day, when it's over-flowing and I attempt to pull the bag out, I end up with a torn bag and garbage all over the floor? Of course, he has his teeny-tiny moments of annoyance with me too. I'll admit that, among other things, I'm not always the most careful person in the entire United States of America when I load the dishwasher and, for the most part, reading instruction booklets is anathema to me.

"This doesn't work!" I'll declare with the petulance of an overtired five-year-old.

"Did you read the instructions?" David asks.

Without waiting for an answer, he fishes around in the bottom of the shipping box for the booklet and gathers the heap of components to the juicer, vacuum cleaner, or whatever new appliance has made its way into our home.

"Let me give it a try," he says. "With the *instructions* this time."

Between infatuation and petty irritation, of course, is the way we experience each other *most of the time*. We are supportive friends and partners in parenting. We are prone to tease each other for our eccentricities, eager for excuses to go out to dinner together, and always happy to open our home to our friends. Needless to say, after twenty-five years, I feel extremely fortunate to be married to David.

Every day of our lives, in some way, shape, or form, we say yes to each other.

We say yes to our children too. I want my children to always hear loud and clear the Yes of our love for them and to be confident, hopeful, and whole. When life hands them the kind of hissing, mortifying No contained in that letter to David so long ago, I want my children to be able to crumple it up, toss it into the garbage can, and move on. In a perfect world, their parents' love would protect them and somehow serve as a shield from mean-spirited people or other disappointments life will certainly deliver. But I know it's not a perfect world. Each of my children will have crushing blows to navigate, no matter how well I manage to nurture, love, and guide them.

So I say yes to them when I can.

Yes, you can ride the mechanical horse at the front of the grocery store until I can't find any more quarters in the bottom of my purse.

Yes, we can go on a walk, play Uno, or color together.

Yes, you can stay up late on a summer night, have a friend sleep over, and skip practicing your viola today.

Yes, you should try out for that.

Yes, I'll take you and your friend to that concert.

Yes, you are old enough, brave enough, and smart enough.

Yes, yes, yes.

It's tricky to walk that tightrope between Yes and No, to know when to reach our hands up and exclaim that fledge word *Yes* or when to direct our hands toward the ground in an angular *No*. As parents, we're faced with that decision countless times a day. *Yes*, you can watch that *Bob the Builder* video. *No*, you can't have a cookie. *Yes*, you can go to the football game with your friends. *No*, you can't have money for that.

Yes, No, Yes, No.

A friend tells me her parenting philosophy is to say to her kids, "Just let the word *no* echo through your heads." She's kidding, of course, but isn't it tempting sometimes to go that route? Parenting is trickier than that, and as we falter along that high-wire act, awkwardly holding whatever we use as our balancing poles, an audience gathers and people begin to point. If we lean too far toward Yes, we're labeled as permissive. When we veer the other direction, we're control freaks or Helicopter Moms. But those labels aren't really accurate, are they? Aren't all of us some combination of all of these as we muddle along as parents?

For example, if you'd seen me as a young mother of three at the grocery store, my four-year-old walking alongside me, my two-year-old sitting in the cart facing me, and the baby in her carrier, maybe you'd have thought me an Earth Mama, wearing a groovy sling and filling the cart with organic sweet potatoes, recycled paper towels, and soy milk. You would have seen the dark circles under my eyes and might have even been one of the countless people who smiled at me and said, "You've got your hands full."

My children, obediently trotting with me into the store, would likely have appealed to you. "What *nice* children," you might have said, smiling at my slightly disheveled but competent-enough mommy self.

But what if you'd heard me lean in to my eldest and whisper, as we entered the store, the same thing I said to him *every single time* we went grocery shopping back then?

"Theo. *Remember*. If you walk along with Mommy and have good behavior, you can pick a new Hot Wheels car when we check out." (If you don't believe me, take a look at the bin of cars in our basement; it worked like a charm.) And what about when my two-year-old, halfway through the store, pointed at a box of graham crackers and, before he even fussed, I had it open, handing him a cracker when I'd not yet even paid? Was I failing to teach him delayed gratification? Would he forever be warped by having his desires met so easily? He'll probably be living in the basement when he's thirty, right? Calling upstairs to demand that I bring him a Pop Tart and fresh batteries for the remote.

Even worse, what about when, on the drive home from the grocery store, you had heard my boys begin chanting "Taco Bell! Taco Bell! Taco Bell"? What if you'd seen me turn the car around and pull into the drive-through line, ordering kid meals for them and nachos bel grande for myself? (What can I say? I had a mad craving for nachos bel grande whenever I was nursing a baby.) Adios, Earth Mama! As I exited the drive-through, I was now Fast-Food-Eating, Permissive, Consumeristic Mom, icily turning a blind eye to the environmental impact of single-use products such as taco wrappers, tinfoil, and junky plastic toys.

The point is, in a culture when we are quick to judge and label others—much as we despise being judged ourselves—we parents experience a lot of anxiety about raising kids. Sadly, we add to it by judging other mothers who are fumbling along just like we are. Worse, mothers these days are expected to do so much. While our counterparts in generations past felt that parenting was primarily about keeping children healthy (that is, *alive and breathing*) so the young ones could, I don't know, be strong enough to help bring in the harvest, milk the cows, and chop firewood, we now feel responsible for everything from helping our children excel at cartwheels and chemistry to preventing them from experiencing disappointment, regret, or failure of any kind. We also feel pressure—regardless of their academic aptitude—to push our children toward wowing their teachers with their smarts. Exposing them to Mandarin Chinese from toddlerhood is also a good idea given the global economy they will someday shape. Additionally, they should be self-possessed, able to laugh at their foibles, physically fit and attractive, and—if you're a person of faith—they should have vital spiritual lives.

Got all that?

We take a deep breath and do our best, trying to balance

Yes and No and learning as we go. But whenever we turn around, someone is poised to judge us, point out our mistakes, and tell us what kind of (bad or ridiculous) mother we are.

Send in store-bought cookies for your kid's birthday treat? You're a Slacker Mom. (You probably don't even know who your kid's teacher is.) Green Mamas dress their kids as wind turbines on Halloween and give out dried figs, bundled in wax paper. A Stage Mom—or, as I recently heard this type of mother called, a *momateur*—lives out her unrealized dreams by pushing her children into the limelight. Helicopter Moms hover, micromanaging their children's lives. The list goes on, blithely turning often well-intentioned moms into caricatures and diminishing all of us.

And who consistently fits the description of one of these types of moms, anyway? Most of us start the day as one thing—Crafty Mom, for instance, with the watercolors and cheery children's music playing—and soon morph in and out of three other types by ten in the morning. Slacker, Martyr, and Epic-Fail Mom, perhaps? I know on any given day, I'm a combination of many types, usually before lunch. Or when they were younger, even before breakfast.

When children are very young, some days seem to go on forever, don't they? The telltale chatter on the baby monitor at five in the morning lets you know your day has started. Several hours and multiple temper tantrums, sticky kisses, dirty diapers, picture books, and time-outs later, you look beseechingly at the clock but find it's not even noon. By five in the afternoon, you've fallen asleep twice while reading with your child, drunk two pots of coffee, and walked furrows into the wood floors while comforting your infant.

I was recently on the phone with a friend who has two young children. It was about six in the evening and she sounded spent.

"Long day?" I asked, although I knew the answer.

"Her new thing is spreading 'fairy dust,'" my friend said.

"That's sweet—"

"'Fairy dust' is whatever's left at the bottom of the cracker box or bag of pretzels. She runs through the house scattering it."

"Oh," I said.

"Yeah," she said with a sigh. "And now we have ants."

I know my friend felt the day would never end.

When my children were very young, I often instituted a game of "Hospital" with them in a desperate ploy to close my eyes for a few moments. "Okay, you're the doctors and nurses and Mommy's the patient. I'll lie here and you can make me all better," I'd say, collapsing onto the sofa. I'd pull a blanket over myself as my young kids busied themselves for five or ten minutes with the toy stethoscope, syringe, and bandages. (Word to the wise—this game can buy a much-needed power nap for parents of preschoolers.) I remember sitting up from the game, covered in Hello Kitty and Batman Band-Aids, having deeply traveled into REM sleep and vivid dreams. I woke up feeling like a new woman.

"Mommy's all better! Thank you, doctors!"

Now, with my kids' ages all in the double digits, I'm no longer in such desperate need for a few moments of rest. For a chunk of the day, the house is quiet. My days go by quickly and, as I repeatedly tell my friends with younger children, it *is* easier. Those long and wearying hands-on days are saved for times when one or more of us is sick.

I find the interpersonal challenges, the chauffeuring, the monitoring of academic and social growth, and the rest of the tasks associated with parenting tweens and teens easier than those *fill the sippy cup and crawl under the table to wipe up the food she's flung from her highchair* days. Of course, there was much to love when my kids were very young. The snuggles and kisses. The dance contests and the fun we had singing together in the car. Reading books together, hour after hour. The way my babies' faces, on seeing my approach, would break into huge smiles as if I was the most welcome sight in the world. I loved feeling little hands reach up and grasp my own. I was delighted by their funny observations and knock-knock-joke marathons.

But, still, I found it exhausting to be "on" all the time. I was too often catapulted into worry. "Will she survive her toddlerhood, given her propensity for hurling herself off the furniture?" "Will he be a perfectionist, never satisfied with his efforts?"

And even though they're older, I still cuddle with my kids. My daughters hold my hands as we walk along the sidewalk or through parking lots. My sons still let me give them kisses and squeezes. But instead of having to lecture them about not using invisible ink on their penmanship homework or advising them of the dangers of licking the chain-link fence at the dog park, we can talk about ideas, current events, music, and books. I love it.

Not all mothers prefer parenting older kids, of course. We all have different resources, gifts, and experiences with our children. But for me, parenting kids who can, say, take care of their own fecal matter and be trusted to cross the street safely feels easier. And all of those yesses and nos of early, relationship-building parenting seem to have brought rewards of real, authentic connection between my children and me.

Are my kids ever sassy or unreasonable? Yes. Do I ever have to ground them, take away their cell phones, or forbid them from going on Facebook until their math grades improve? Yes, of course. Do I ever think, *Who in the world is this person and why is he glaring at me?* Yes, yes. But in this imperfect world, my kids and I generally live in peace. We trust and enjoy each other. They confide in me about their friends, hopes, and failings. My heart often does a little somersault when they get home at the end of the school day.

And thanks to chore lists, I rarely have to do my most dreaded household tasks, such as pairing socks, vacuuming the stairs, or filling the dog's food bowl. When my four children were very little, it never occurred to me that someday they would not only shower by themselves but be capable of serving themselves a bowl of cereal. Now they are actually pitching in to the running of our household. I'm grateful. (Hey, kids, quit your complaining. It's not like you have to milk the cows at four in the morning—or, for that matter, drink powered milk!)

"It does get better," I tell my friend with the fairy-dust-spreading daughter. "I promise."

All of a sudden, I'm aware that the clock is ticking and my remaining time with children at home is short. Instead of watching the clock and wishing the days away, things sneak up on me. My son's first girlfriend. (*Wait? Girlfriend? Do we have a policy on this?*) Puberty! (*Honey, you need to teach him how to shave!*) The fact that my oldest is two years away from college. (*College? But didn't he just learn to ride his two-wheeler?*) Before long my children will be responsible to make *all their own* choices about the people with whom they build relationships and about who they want to be in this world. They will have to decide when to say no and when to lift their hands in a big, fledgy yes.

It can be daunting to think about, but moms wiser than me offer hope.

A friend of mine, Virginia, is mother to one child. Virginia's daughter is now an adult; she has graduated from college and lives in a different state than her parents. Virginia and I recently talked about how our perception of time shifts midway through parenting our kids. That is, time seems to drag on when we are caring for the needs of babies and young children, but then—*poof!*—suddenly the children are in middle school. We notice the hair on our sons' upper lips. Our daughters start wearing clothes from the juniors' department. *When did that baby fat disappear, leaving us with these tall, lean kids? When did the stuffed animals disappear from their beds? Where did the past few years go?* It all feels like a blur.

We begin to look with a more deliberate gaze at how we want these last years to go with our children at home. What do we want them to remember? Are there vacations, traditions, or anything else that we want to embrace in a big Yes? What have we left out, failed to share with them, missed?

"I used to worry," my friend Virginia said. "I used to think that the clock strikes twelve when they turn eighteen and then it's over. But it's not like that at all. I love this new time in our relationship. We are as close as we ever were. I shouldn't have worried."

I drink in her words.

Playwright Jean Anouilh wrote in his drama *Antigone*, "To say yes, you have to sweat and roll up your sleeves and plunge both hands into life up to the elbows."

That sounds a lot like family life to me, with all its challenges, perspiration, and promise.

CHAPTER 2

The Body Hair Incident
Adventures in Accepting Conflict

My longsuffering neighbor must have heaved a great sigh of relief when my family and I moved away and she was no longer the object of a young mom's focused attention. She could take her dog on a walk in peace without seeing a shadow pass behind the window across the street, the red front door open, and my sudden appearance on the front porch.

"Oh, hi! Got a minute?" I used to call.

Now, a decade later, *I'm* the one driving a van, pulling in and out of my garage multiple times a day. *My* kids are the big kids now, the kids at whom—when they amble through the park and nostalgically climb up on a rope bridge on the playground equipment—the mothers of preschoolers sometimes glare, drawing their children a bit closer to them.

I used to do the same thing. When your children are still teetering along on unsteady legs and you see even a few perfectly well-mannered fourth graders enter the perimeter of the park, your defenses go up.

Who are those big people?

What are they doing in proximity to my darling little child?

What if they knock her over?

What if they curse or tell an inappropriate joke?

Shouldn't they be at work or something?

As I'm sure my former neighbor predicted but was too kind to mention, over the past several years I've been baptized by fire (and sassiness and exhaustion and disappointment) into the ragged, crazy-making world of raising kids. Parenting sure is messier than I expected it would be. Although I've gotten to the point where I can take a breath and know that it's not the end of the world when things go awry in our home, hanging on to that sense of calm is sometimes still a struggle for me.

Not too long ago, for instance, I dedicated a Sunday afternoon to creating a picture-perfect family night. The week ahead would be busy; I wanted the six of us to have a chance to connect with each other before it began. Using perfectly ripe tomatoes from my husband's garden, fresh mozzarella, and baby spinach, I made a savory tart that my family loves. I baked a carrot cake from scratch, for the first time using a top-secret recipe given to me by someone who must remain nameless. (If I *were* to share her name, you'd agree that she could only be considered an expert on such matters. No, it is not Sara Lee or Betty Crocker, but someone along those lines.) Of all the carrot cakes I've ever made— and I've made a number of them—this was the best. It was a triumph, topped with delicious homemade cream-cheese icing. Things were shaping up for an idyllic night.

But, that evening, after we spent hours together, chatting over dinner and raucously playing Rock Band on the Wii, my sons stumbled into an argument that quickly turned bitter. I was getting out dessert plates and getting ready to cut the glorious cake when it happened. My husband was also out of the room, loading the dishwasher. One son said that every part of the body had hair on it. The other pointed out that the palms of the hands as well as eyeballs—and a lot of other places (Fingernails, anyone?)—most certainly do *not* sprout hair. A debate ensued on whether, when he said "every part" of the body, my son meant *every single part* or simply *every major area* of the body. And what about those tiny fine hairs, like in the nose, that you can only barely see? Could there be body hairs so minuscule and fair that they are invisible to the naked eye? On your eyeballs?

The argument was gaining momentum; I attempted to knock it off course.

"Sometimes when I get a pedicure, the woman shaves the tops of my big toes," I called from the kitchen. "It makes me feel like a hobbit."

My comment was ignored, and the quarrel continued, spiraling down into a nasty place. The boys dragged their younger sisters into it: one took one brother's side, the other joined forces with the other. Insults, dark looks, and generalizations were tossed around the room.

"You *always* talk about things you know *nothing* about!"

"Why do you *always* pick at me like this?"

"Why do you *always* think you're right?"

One son muttered a coarse word his sister had never heard him say and she dissolved into tears.

When my husband and I returned to the family room, the air was electric with anger and hurt. Three of the four kids were in tears. All this over body hair. (Or the lack of it.)

Now, never mind that I'm in my forties. Never mind that I'd been a parent for fifteen years. Never mind that, as a columnist who frequently writes about raising children, I know that this kind of inane bickering is an inevitable part of family life. Never mind all the work I've done to face down and let go of my own childhood issues. Despite all of that, coming upon this tangled-up scene felt like a missile to my heart, leaving it burning, exposed, and raw. My face flushed; hot tears filled my eyes.

In high school, I went to an amusement park with friends. On one ride, passengers were ushered into a circular room and told to stand against the walls. The ride started to spin and our bodies were forced to the wall and, spinning much faster, the floor dropped out from below our feet. Only centrifugal force kept us suspended.

When my kids are entangled in a nasty argument like that, I occasionally feel like I'm on that ride again, the room spinning, the odd sensation of the floor disappearing from under my feet. I fear that all of our happiness, all of the work I've done to create a certain kind of family culture, is falling down like a house of cards in the wind.

This. Isn't. Supposed. To. Happen. We have a happy, loving family. We are generous with each other. What have I done wrong? Haven't I modeled peace and tolerance? Don't they know that the greatest commandment is to love God and others? This isn't loving. This isn't happy. Weren't we all just having a marvelous time three minutes ago? What happened to our happy evening?

But being a parent means being brave and, you know, punting one's own childhood trauma out the door once in a while and just dealing with whatever's at hand. Several years ago I might have run up to my bedroom in tears, leaving my husband and kids puzzled and concerned. But now, happily, I've matured at least a little bit and, however imperfectly, have learned to stay in the room to help guide us out of such quagmires.

I took a breath.

"Come on, everyone. We need to talk," I said.

We retreated to the living room to work things out. The girls sat sniffling. One son sat at the edge of the room, his arms folded and eyes glowering. The other sat facing the wall. I said I'd worked hard on making a big night and wish they hadn't been so small to each other. (Cue the maternal guilt and violin music.) At this, my husband suggested that one of the boys had overreacted and I, champion of the free expression of emotions, took issue with that.

"How can you know that someone is *overreacting*? Only *he* knows how that felt to him," I snapped.

Despite the rocky start, after a few minutes feelings were patched up. Those who were angry or hurt expressed why they felt that way. The son who said the coarse word (though technically not a swear word) apologized that he had offended his sister, but said he felt it was the only word that adequately expressed his frustration at that particular moment.

I calmed down and backpedaled from the tiresome "Look at all I've done for you today and this is what I get?" mode and into a more helpful "Everyone has misunderstandings like this; it's part of life" set of remarks and a short pep talk about family. The kids apologized to each other for being rude. Somehow the whole body hair discussion fell by the wayside and was no longer relevant.

With the emotional mess sufficiently tidied up, we ate the cake.

That night, as I said good night to my eldest child, Theo, he apologized to me for his part in what had happened.

"You know, this kind of stuff feels worse to everyone in our family because it's rare," he said. "If it happened more often, we'd be used to it and it wouldn't feel like such a big deal."

"You're right," I said. And of course he was.

I've come to recognize that at off-kilter times like the night of the Body Hair Incident when I feel like the floor is spinning, my childhood scars are flaring up. At those moments, I need to step away, take a breath, and refocus. A friend of mine says her son, on seeing that her anxiety level is rising fast, calmly says, "We count to ten when we're upset, Mama. Just take a deep breath and count to ten." Over the years, I've managed to do that more. Count to ten. Breathe. Refocus.

I no longer think I can flutter above conflict like a fairy godmother. I no longer think I can raise my children without ever letting them down, misunderstanding them, or failing them. I know they'll argue, I'll lose my temper, and sometimes we'll have to retreat again to the other room to repair our relationships. I no longer worry that every bad day is the beginning of the end for us as a family. Kids *will* argue about body hair. I *will* sometimes lose my temper and want to jump up and down like a child. I *will* make the mistake of looking too far into the future, fearing that the white lie she just told makes her destined for a life of deceit. When one of the kids is sick I *will* lose perspective, tumble into despair, and believe that I'll never have another night of undisturbed sleep again. I *will* be inconsistent. I *will* take things personally even when I know I shouldn't. I *will* get involved in my children's arguments instead of remembering to let them try to work things out. Now at least, I can regain my equilibrium a lot sooner than I could a decade ago.

So that's progress, right?

As David and I walked out of the theater, he turned to me and asked, "So, did you ever think you'd see a movie that would so closely resemble your life?" The smile fell from my face. I looked around in hopes that no one, even though they were strangers, had heard what he said. Thoughts stomped into my head, noisily, like kids running in the back door and letting the screen door slam.

My life, like the movie Motherhood?

Uma Thurman plays its central character, Eliza, so that's flattering enough. And despite the fact that the movie gives us a day in Eliza's life that, if anything, is *Alexander and the Terrible, Horrible, No Good, Very Bad Day* for mommies, her character manages to keep her sense of humor, most of the time. I should have been grateful for the comparison, right? But I live in a colonial-style house in the suburbs of Chicago, not a walk-up in Manhattan's Greenwich Village. I have four children; Eliza has two. My children have outgrown their sippy cups, so I no longer quench my thirst by stealing a swig from such things.

Wait, though—like Eliza, my bookshelves hold literary journals that contain writing I did twenty-something years ago, heavily symbolic poems and stories that drip with meaning. And it's true that I often steal out of the room and hunch over my laptop in the kitchen as the boys play FIFA soccer on the Wii or the girls play a board game on the floor of the family room.

The first part of the movie, comprised of comic scenes in which Eliza muddles hour by hour and task by task through her morning, seems almost unbelievably over the top. The myriad details involved in getting kids ready for school would seem overstated if I hadn't lived through many such days myself. And as Eliza, Sherpa-like, makes her way home from the store laden with boxes and bags after getting supplies for her daughter's birthday party, the filmmaker adds a nice touch. Around her neck, further weighing her down—and bringing to mind Dickens' Jacob Marley from *A Christmas Carol*—is a thick, steel bike chain.

Then there's the scene in which Eliza almost snaps and for a moment actually thinks about fleeing the reality of her life to escape to New Jersey. As she drives, looking panicked and desperate, I turned to my husband and whispered, "Oh, I know just what she is feeling."

I did; it made my chest hurt.

Throughout the movie, I kept thinking, *No one talks about all of this—and certainly, in a feature film no one depicts the experience of raising children.* The extreme highs and lows that can occur every single day as a parent. The worry that sometimes buzzes and sometimes howls with the message that you are losing your identity. The mind-numbing number of details to manage. The way your heart crumbles and melts inside you when you are able to see through all the craziness for a moment and fall in love with your child again.

Not long ago, I was driving home at the end of a long day. In front of me was a man on a motorcycle. As I followed him through an intersection, we passed another motorcycle going the opposite direction. As they passed each other, the second rider raised his hand to the guy in front of me in a show of solidarity. The man in front of me returned the wave. The simple fact that they both were driving motorcycles was enough for them to feel a connection and greet each other.

I pulled into my driveway a few minutes later and remembered that exchange with envy. Imagine being accepted, greeted—seen!—simply because of the vehicle you were driving. It occurred to me that, in a perfect world, we mothers should do the same. As we pass each other in our minivans with our mutual silhouettes of kids in the backseats, our windows revealing the messy undersides of their sticker collages, we should make eye contact, raise our hands, and wave just to salute the other person to indicate that we *see* each other and that we are on the same journey as mothers.

Maybe it would serve as an acknowledgment that when the other mother reminds her child to say "please" and "thank you" for the tenth time that day or patiently answers questions about whether fish sleep or where the moon goes during the day or how to spell *Mississippi*—despite how exhausted she is or the worries on her mind—she is doing something meaningful. Unnoticed, perhaps. Thankless, usually. But she is, by these simple acts, teaching her child about what it means to live in a community and about what the world is like. Perhaps, most importantly, her actions teach her child that the child matters and is worth being heard.

I know, I know. All that waving and smiling might result in a spate of minivan collisions. But on our way to playgroup, the grocery store, or the park, we aren't exactly tearing up the streets, are we? These will be minor fender benders and—who knows?—maybe we'll end up making a few new friends.

"Were you waving at me? Was something wrong?"

"I just waved to let you know *I see you*."

"What?"

"I'm in the same line of work. *Mommying*. And I wanted you to know I appreciate you."

"Really?"

"Yes, really. Now you have to tell me where you found that car seat . . ."

By the way, *Motherhood* (which, in the end, I had to agree with David was eerily similar to my life) was hardly a box-office triumph. Released in 2009, it grossed something like $100,000 globally. Maybe its anticipated audience was too busy changing diapers, making peanut butter and jelly sandwiches, and folding laundry to notice that there was a new movie out about them.

But as for me, I took comfort in it. It felt like that wished-for wave of acknowledgment that what I'm doing as a parent is real and it is hard. Because, after all, we don't wave at the other moms in the minivans or pushing the grocery cart next to us, do we? We walk past the mom with the whiny toddler in her cart, and instead of remembering that our child whined last week too or seeing that she is wearing that same Jacob Marley chain around her neck that we are, we judge her.

Why can't she just show a little authority? we wonder.

Does she not know that her child's wailing and screeching grates on the nerves of everyone in earshot?

What's her problem?

We don't think of her as the real person she is. A real person with a real life and real burdens to bear. She might have just learned that someone she loves has been diagnosed with cancer. Or that her husband has left her. Or maybe she is moving through the aisles of the store worrying that when she swipes her credit card, it will be declined and she'll have to leave the cartful of food behind. Again.

Or maybe she is just having a perfectly ordinary, terrible day.

Maybe if we were to see her in the grocery store the next week, we'd witness her child singing a sweet song or reaching his arms up to embrace her whenever she gets close to him. Maybe seeing the joyful way she and her child *usually* interact with each other would inspire us as parents.

You never know.

Returning to the night of the Body Hair Incident, before they went up to bed, I asked my kids to stop and look around the room. As they did so, puzzled and a little bemused, I launched into a kind of impromptu Saint Crispin's Day speech. If you aren't a fan of Shakespeare's plays and don't know the reference, the speech is found in *Henry V*. Henry addresses his ragtag troops before the Battle of Agincourt, inspiring them to an unlikely victory against the French.

He says,

We few, we happy few, we band of brothers;
For he to-day that sheds his blood with me
Shall be my brother; be he ne'er so vile,
. . . And gentlemen in England now-a-bed
Shall think themselves accurs'd they were not here,
And hold their manhoods cheap whiles any speaks
That fought with us upon Saint Crispin's day.

(Act IV, Scene 3)

The Saint Crispin's Day speech never fails to bring tears to my eyes. I know, I know: I'm a sap. The point is, my own unplanned speech that night had, now that I look back on it, a bit of a "we few, we happy few" vibe.

As they looked around the room at the faces of each of their siblings, I said, "These, for better and worse, are your people. These are the cast of characters in your lives. You'll have other people too—friends and husbands and wives and children of your own—but these people will always matter to you, even if you wish they didn't. Let's make this home a safe place for each other. Let's enjoy each other as much as possible while we're all living together in this house. Treat each other with respect. Cut each other some slack. Look for what's good in each other. What do you say?"

When they were much younger, this would have been the point at which I would have gathered them into a huddle and done a cheer. "Hands in, everyone!" I used to shout. But given that I had two teenage sons and two tween girls eying me warily, I resisted the urge.

So, although I give the occasional corny speech and although I am prone to taking my kids' quarrels too seriously and although my own childhood issues sometimes cloud my good sense, I'm doing my level best. Truly, I've even come to be *grateful* that my hopes for maternal perfection have been dashed both by my own failings and by my kids' extraordinarily ordinary clashes with each other. Ugly arguments over the relative talent of Ke$ha. Conflict over who unloads the dishwasher most often. And, of course, the presence or absence of hair on various parts of the body.

I'm thankful in part because had I not been disabused of the myth of the perfect family, I might have become obsessed with protecting and maintaining my version of it. I might have been compulsively obsessed with it, really, and may have unwittingly joined a cult that, despite its often benign intentions, can be sinister and can close us off from engaging with the wider world. That cult, of course, is the cult of family. As a person who longed for a functional family as a child, I was primed to put on the robes, chime the hand cymbals, hang out at the airport handing out daisies, and join the cult of family as a lifetime member. Instead, thanks to the fact that I've had to butt up against real life, I see my own family as a ragtag bunch who, for a time, share a home, create memories together, and grow with each other. Together we are learning to love as the shine is rubbed off of our backs, and we increasingly become Real.

CHAPTER 3

Mommy Misdemeanors
Adventures in Messing Up

My sister-in-law is a terrific mother.

Wait—let me back up. *All three* of my sisters-in-law are wonderful mothers, but I'd like to share a story with you about the one who's not named Julie and whose children are still very young. Both of my brothers married women named Julie. (So did my father, but that is a story for another day.) My sisters-in-law, the Julies, are terrific mothers. Both of them have four children and one of them is a foster mother who welcomes children into her home for days, weeks, and even months at a time. The other Julie is one of the most resilient people I know who—when faced with academic, medical, or any other challenge that presents itself to her family—grits her teeth, does her research, and labors to remove it. My brothers did very well by marrying the Julies.

But Sara, my other sister-in-law—*not a Julie*—is also an exceptional mother. If you knew her, you'd agree. She is married to my husband's brother and lives in Cambridge, Massachusetts. She is deliberate about the food her three young children eat. (*Organic blueberries! Cage-free eggs!*) She makes outdoor play such a part of her kids' lives that they consider their neighborhood park a second home. She gives her children clear boundaries, and she lavishes generous heaps of love on them every single day.

To make matters better—or worse if you are already overcome with jealousy over her mothering prowess, as I have been—she used cloth diapers exclusively for years, avoids paper towels and other single-use products (unlike her naughty sister-in-law going through the Taco Bell drive-through lane and shamelessly buying Pampers Mega Packs back in the day), teaches her children sign language when they are babies, and seems only mildly annoyed when the stacks of wooden puzzles in her house make sounds when slightly jostled or when the lights go down. (What's with that, by the way?)

Recently she sent me an e-mail in which she confessed she had failed that day as a mom. My interest was piqued—really? *Failed?* I will include a part of that e-mail here for one very important reason; and that is, every one of us—let me stop and be perfectly clear: *each and every one of us*—judges ourselves too harshly, thinks we've failed, and holds ourselves to impossible standards, ones to which we would never, ever, ever hold another person. Even someone for whom we have little respect! Seriously. (By the way, yes of course, there are moms who truly neglect and abuse their children, and such moms aren't ones whom I'd encourage to go easier on themselves as parents . . . but my guess is that these women aren't perusing the "Parenting and Childcare" section of the bookstore in their spare time.)

Okay, now that we've cleared all that up, here is what Sara wrote:

Had a real freak-out this morning. Not at the kids, thank goodness, but in their presence. Nutty morning, and then nowhere to park. I ended up yelling at a traffic officer (through the glass, not like she could hear me) and I think it stressed the kids out a bit. Not pretty and not proud. Lessons learned.

Now I don't mean to belittle the stress Sara was under that morning. She has three kids, ages five and younger. She is in graduate school. Her husband works long hours. And did I mention the cloth diapers and those puzzles that honk and beep or make animal noises if you so much as tiptoe past them?

Sara and I have been sisters-in-law for sixteen years. I count her as one of the people I most admire. But I wanted to say, "Shouting at a police officer through the glass? That's *nothing.*" I don't mean that she should have jumped from the car and taken all of her frustration, exhaustion, and rage out on the poor traffic cop. I also don't mean that she wasn't, like Uma Thurman's character in *Motherhood*, half a sippy cup away from having an emotional meltdown of epic proportions. I remember how hard it is in the hands-on phase of parenting in which she and my brother-in-law reside.

As my friend Seth, the father of two very young kids, says, "They *break terrorists* with more sleep than this."

No, I just mean that every good parent I know has messed up, served as a bad example to his or her children, and then thought, *I am the worst mother (or father) in the world.* I know I have. I don't shrug off my own shortcomings. I hope, as much as possible, to demonstrate the fruit of the spirit—love, joy, peace, patience, kindness, goodness, faithfulness, gentleness, and self-control—in my parenting (Galatians 5:22 CEB). I hope to be attentive to my kids, but not to stifle them. Kind, without being saccharine-sweet. Gentle and patient, but not blasé. Devoted to my faith, but not falsely pious. You know, a healthy balance of sweet and salty, crunchy and soft. Kind of like kettle corn.

But I fail; we all do.

All of us commit misdemeanors. We lose our tempers. We look away from the baby for a moment at the precise second when he learns to roll over, and then, horrified, watch him fall from the changing table. We've all tucked a watercolor painting or crayon drawing deep underneath the newspaper in the recycling bin only later to learn it was her "best ever" and she was going to ask to have it framed. (Meanwhile we hear the recycling truck idling half a block away, the treasure crumpled and torn somewhere below its enormous jaws.) We've all done things like showing up late to a soccer game and missing his only goal of the season or misjudging a situation and punishing our child for something she didn't do.

(Or maybe that's just me.)

This section is going to be fun.

I solicited "Bad Mommy" stories from my friends. I won't include identifying details for most of them because I promised I wouldn't. But I hope that reading these anecdotes will ease my sister-in-law Sara's conscience next time she is having an "I'm the worst mom in the world" moment, and I hope it will ease your troubled mind too.

The Pokémon Sticker

When my son Theo was three, I broke up with American culture. We did eventually reconcile, but with new rules about the relationship. (That story follows, in chapter 6.) For now, suffice it to say that it seemed to me that every time I turned around, advertisers were trying to sell me—and, worse, my kids—not only a bunch of toys and other items that had "Planned for Obsolescence" stamped into their undersides but the notion that the more stuff we crammed into our home, the happier we would be.

As a person who's concerned about the environment, a bit of a neat freak, and most importantly as a person of faith, I wanted to reject that message.[1] And rejecting it takes work. Which one of us doesn't enjoy paging through a Crate and Barrel holiday catalog or the momentary thrill of the UPS man running up the sidewalk to deliver a Zappos box containing her new shoes? (Let she who is without sin cast the first stone.) Still, I wanted to do what I could to raise children who wouldn't blithely accept that whoever has the most toys in the end wins, despite the numerous times we are spoon-fed that idea by our culture.

The breakup climaxed in the moment when I yanked our television cord from the wall. I decided that in their early, impressionable years, I would limit my kids' exposure to commercial messages. (This was in the late 1990s: pre-TiVo, Netflix streaming, and other technology that has since allowed viewers more control over what they see. Watching television back then meant sitting through commercials. Lots of them.)

I also wanted my children to have playthings that, as much as possible, weren't mass-produced and destined for a landfill. I even requested white PVC pipe (with connectors, elbows, and rings) from my husband's longsuffering parents for Theo's birthday when he was in preschool. He could, you know, build with them. And then when he was done, we could use the pipes for leaks under the sink or, I don't know, an irrigation system should we ever decide to dig one.

Did I mention I had four children in six years? I was exhausted. And yes, Seth, terror suspects in detention camps get more sleep than do the parents of young children.[2] (In a related matter, did you know that the "I love you, you love me" theme song from *Barney and Friends* really *has* been used to break terrorists?[3])

When Theo went to preschool, the menacing (okay, to be honest, they were wonderful) teachers were always subverting my plan to keep his mind and spirit free of junk culture. They showed cartoons on rainy days. There were Happy Meal toys in the sandbox. Everywhere we went, I felt that people were desperately working to get him hooked on the junk I was so intent on avoiding. Even the pediatrician and dentist gave out character stickers after visits. There I was, trying to be a responsible parent with our annual physicals and biannual teeth cleanings, and yet I had to deal with blaring TV screens in the waiting room.

Most of the time, I was able to guide Theo's choice of I WENT TO THE DENTIST TODAY or I HAD MY SHOTS TODAY stickers. There were always acceptable choices—pictures of pandas or dinosaurs. But there were always branded, character stickers as well. Disney princesses. Bart Simpson. SpongeBob.

"What's that?" Theo would ask, pointing to that starfish guy from *SpongeBob SquarePants*.

"No idea," I'd say, acting disinterested and sighing as though it were the most boring and irrelevant thing I'd ever seen in my entire life.

One day, however, after a checkup at the dentist, I let my guard down. I must have been distracted for a moment by chatting with the hygienist or by keeping my younger children from escaping out the door when Theo chose his sticker from the little basket at reception.

"Look what I got! Look!" he shouted. "*Pokémon!*"

Pokémon, of course, is the name of the game, not the character. I believe the character was Pikachu, which is a fun word to say. But to Theo, all of the characters were simply "Pokémon."

Pokémon. My heart fell. I was sure this was the chink that would cause the fortress I'd been building to come crumbling down. Mozart Wednesdays. Library books. Wooden toys. All my efforts, my deliberate parenting, would be gobbled up by those monsters.

It wasn't easy being me.

If you're thinking that I should have lightened up a bit back then, all I can say is, "Absolutely!" Or as my brother Drew and I used to say, "No duh!" But, as I mentioned before, I'd been dreaming of raising children since I was a child myself. I had been full of ideas, hope, and anxiety about being a wife and mother for so long that I wanted, more than anything, to do it right. And, um, I never did find the instruction manual in the bottom of that shipping box telling me the correct way to raise a child.

To be honest, I didn't know much of anything about Pokémon, but what I did know was that it felt like every time I turned around, the people who marketed Pokémon were on the prowl to sell it to my kids and me. It was on toddler underwear, wristwatches, and pajamas. Even worse, one of the other moms at Theo's preschool had told me, as we chatted in the hallway, that she believed those critics of Pokémon who said it was designed to be addictive.

"I read that some kids don't even want to play with their friends anymore after they're addicted," the woman said. "And I can see that. When I tell him it's time to stop, it's like I'm taking away his *drugs*. It's like he's going to go into *withdrawal*. And every time I go to the store, he demands that I get him more trading cards."

I found her report alarming; it strengthened my resolve.

"I wish we'd never started with it," the mom said, shrugging. "But what are you going to do?"

I knew what *I* was going to do—keep that big, bad wolf out of my house, that's what.

Fast-forward a few weeks and there was my sweet little Theo, his T-shirt and his very innocence sullied by the Pokémon sticker from the dentist. My right arm twitched. I wanted to grab it, rip it into shreds, and maybe take him to the opera or on a nature walk. Just to clear his cultural palette. But in a moment of temporary sanity, I paused.

"Oh, that's nice, Theo," I said.

I let it go. I was so proud of myself. *It's only a sticker*, I thought. A sticker. He can go home and play with his toy knights or his chess set or his PVC pipes and then, at the end of the day, the sticker will be tossed in the hamper with the rest of the dirty clothes. I can put up with it for a few hours, can't I?

I was proud of myself for being so sensible.

But on arriving home, my mood shifted. As the kids ate lunch, my gaze kept returning to the Pokémon sticker. It cheapened him somehow, turned my son into an advertisement for a product I didn't even like, one that may very well have been created to keep children from interacting with other human beings! I felt my anxiety level rising.

While I cleared the lunch dishes, Theo and Ian played with their cars on the floor near the table. (The PVC pipes never got much play, to be honest. In case you were wondering, we never had cause to build an irrigation system.) At one point, as I glanced into the room, Theo grabbed Ian's hand and roughly grabbed a toy truck his brother was holding.

"Hey, that's *mine*," he said.

Ian began to cry.

I rushed to the boys, took the tiny cement mixer and put it back into Ian's hand, and kneeled down to talk to Theo.

"We don't do that. You know that," I started. "We share in our family."

"That one's mine," he insisted. "Mine!"

In a flash of anger, I reached out and tore the Pokémon sticker off his shirt.

"I knew it. You see?" I sputtered. "You get *this* and suddenly you are ugly to your brother. Suddenly this new side comes out of you and . . ."

As I spoke, I folded the sticker in half and then in half again. I kept on folding it tightly until it was just a tiny pie-shaped ball of paper. I then went to the kitchen garbage can and threw it out.

Theo, all of four years old, stared at me, wide-eyed.

"My Pokémon sticker," he said, tears covering his cheeks.

Yanking the sticker off of Theo's shirt was a "fail" for a mother who seeks to model gentleness and love to her children. The defeated look on his face and the violence with which I grabbed—and then destroyed—his sticker filled me with guilt.

Had I broken his trust forever?

Was I a control freak?

Would Pokémon be the forbidden fruit that, in later life, he somehow traded his innocence for?

When Theo was ten, I asked him if he remembered when I wrecked his sticker. He listened, amused, as I told him the story.

"Hm. Nope. I don't remember that," he said.

Relief washed over me, and I finally—six years after the fact—let go of the nugget of guilt I'd been holding on to ever since the moment I seized that sticker from his shirt. The way his expression went from worried to heartbroken as I folded that sticker over and over onto itself. His big hazel eyes, dripping with tears.

Theo has a wry sense of humor. He also loves to play on my gullibility, a trait I inherited from my mother who, day after day and year after year, never quite figured out when we were kids that my brother and I really didn't see a rabbit or cardinal in the backyard every night. (Sorry, Mom!) But now I'm getting a "taste of my own medicine," as my mother used to say. Every year or so since I told Theo about the destruction of his Pokémon sticker, my son has used the story as an opportunity to tease me. He'll stand quietly in a room with me, looking out a window or into the middle distance.

"Theo? Honey? Are you okay?" I'll ask.

He stands very still.

"Sweetie? What's on your mind?"

He turns to me, and, in the most disheartened tone he can muster, says, "Oh, nothing. I'm just remembering my Pokémon sticker."

He then, of course, bursts into laughter.

The Nap-and-Monitor Charade

A friend of mine lives near to her kids' elementary school. When her younger child was a baby and the elder was in afternoon kindergarten, she occasionally napped when her baby was sleeping. When she started to tell me her "bad mommy" story, she was quick to say she didn't nap often and that it was just for a short period of time, on days when she had finished the laundry or already had dinner started. All the baby books tell us to "sleep when your child sleeps," but have you noticed how *guilty* most of us feel when we take a nap? We say we "just needed to rest our eyes," or we "snuck a nap," when indeed we were desperate for a few moments of quiet and so tired that our eyes were closing without our being able to do anything about it.

(Nap with impunity, moms. You deserve it!)

So my friend would set the alarm on her cell phone for a half hour, fall into a deep sleep, and, once or twice, sleep right through the buzzing. It was not the alarm, but her landline ringing that eventually woke her up. (It was the school calling.) She jumped up from the sofa, grabbed the baby monitor (knowing full well that it wouldn't have reception all the way to the school), and ran down the block to pick up her son. As she jogged along, she held the monitor to her ear, play-acting that she was listening in. Now before you call the authorities, you should know her home is in plain view of the school, and she was gone fewer than five minutes as she ran and picked up her forlorn child from the school office. But she felt, in her words, like an Epic-Fail Mom.

Was she?

I certainly don't think so. Rested, she was likely better able to extend patience and good humor to her kids for the remainder of the day.

Baby's Wild Ride

A friend of mine who is a single dad used to work from home. When his son was a baby, my friend's son would play at his feet. The baby wasn't yet walking but crawled around the floor and played with toys as my friend sat at his desk in his upstairs office, trying to get a full day's work done despite frequent interruptions, bottle breaks, and diaper changes. During that period, his day began earlier and ended much later than a traditional workday and my friend never quite felt caught up with his job. But it was of utmost importance to him to spend time with his son, and the cost of daycare was prohibitive.

He recalls one day being lost in his work and hearing a soft knocking sound. He ignored it, thinking it was a rattle in the heating system or some other household noise. Then, after a few minutes, he looked up and was alarmed to find that the baby was no longer playing in the room with him. He ran to the stairs—a steep set—and saw that the baby gate hadn't been latched properly. His son was at the bottom of the steps, lying on his side and playing with the laces on a pair of shoes. My friend says he never took a set of stairs in so few steps. He examined the boy, was amazed that he was unharmed, and then sat shaking for an hour as he imagined what could have happened.

The child is now eleven years old and seems to have no lasting physical or emotional impairment from his tumble down the steps. They're durable and made to last, these kids.

The Injured Booty

"I was a bad mom this week," my friend said, blinking away tears. "Really bad."

She and I sat at the picnic table in her yard. Our children played on the swings and ran around us. Her three daughters had intermittently caught her up in hugs, shouted for her to watch some trick they wanted to perform, and laughed together.

Whatever she'd done, I could tell, hadn't caused permanent damage.

"That's hard for me to believe," I said.

Theo, then about seven years old, came to the table and sat with us, ever interested in adult conversation.

"I was trying to get the baby down for her nap, but her sister kept waking her up. She was singing at full voice and kept stomping around upstairs. I told her to stop it, to let her sister sleep, but every time I turned around, she was back upstairs jumping around. Finally I took her by the hand and sat her down on the bottom step for a time-out. I got right in her face and growled at her, 'Your baby sister needs her nap. How many times have I told you to be quiet?'"

Telling the story, my friend put her face in her hands.

"Hey, that's not being a bad mom. You were frustrated," I said. "I'm sure I've done something like that a dozen times. Haven't I, Theo?"

He nodded.

"But then she started crying, this pathetic cry that went on and on. Her face was covered in tears," my friend said. "I asked her what was wrong and she said, 'You sat me down too hard. That hurt my booty.' I felt like a child abuser."

Right then that same daughter was clamoring across the monkey bars on their play set. "Hey, Mom! Mom, Mom, Mom—look! Look at me!" she shouted.

"She seems fine now," I said.

"I feel awful. I hadn't even realized I'd been rough. I even checked her bottom later on to make sure she didn't have a bruise. Thank God—she didn't. I just couldn't believe I'd be so rough with her."

"You know," Theo said, "think of all the times you *didn't* do anything like that. You're usually really gentle. I've seen you. What matters is *most of the time*."

"That's right," I said. "Think of all the times you *didn't* lose your temper. Think of all the times you handled things *right*. What matters is *most of the time*."

Breaking the Baby Doll's Neck

Another woman confessed to me that, in the throes of a Mommy Temper Tantrum,* she inadvertently broke the neck of her daughter's favorite baby doll. The mom had been tidying the house and happened to be holding the doll when her little girl spoke to her in a demanding, bratty tone. In a flash of indignation, before she even realized what she was doing, the mom hurled the doll to the ground. Looking down at it, she saw that the doll's head was cocked strangely to the side; its neck was broken. She hadn't even been thinking of what she was holding, just threw it down

---

Mom-ee Tem-per Tan-truhm. Part of speech: *noun*. Definition: *fit, sudden emotion, frenzy.* (Committed by, um, the maternal unit of the family.)

the way a person might slam a door or stomp her feet when she's upset.

"*Baby Connie?*" her daughter said, her voice suddenly sounding very much like the sweet five-year-old she usually was.

"Oh, she's fine, honey," the mom said, concealing her shock over what she'd done. She then created a diversion, lifted the doll carefully from the floor, and held it by the back of the head to mask its injury. She apologized to her daughter for losing her temper, reminded her to speak to others with respect, and—at her first opportunity—ran out to buy an identical doll to replace Baby Connie. She quietly disposed of the doll with the broken neck, ashamed of the homicide she had committed.

More than a decade later, she still replays that moment of rage, and she regrets it.

Desecrating Theo's sticker was just one of countless sins I've committed as a mother. The one that is not so very dramatic, but fills me with the most shame, is when I fail to listen and truly be present with my children. It's the crime I most frequently commit.

I also can be crabby and unreasonable.

And don't even ask about how our tooth fairy myth has evolved over the years to accommodate the fact that I so often forget to slip change under their pillows on the night a tooth has been lost.

"She's traveling overseas!"

"She doesn't work on Tuesdays! I bet she'll come tonight!"

"She must have put it over here!" And surreptitiously pulling change from my pocket and slipping it under a stuffed owl, I announce, "Look, here it is!"

Additional items on my "bad mommy" rap sheet include:

- Volunteering my children to serve as acolytes or readers at church, or—worse—to play a role in the annual Christmas pageant ("I'm fourteen years old and I'm . . . the angel Gabriel?" my son cried. "I have to wear a dress? And a gold headband?")
- Grounding my older kids for crimes that I later discover they did not commit
- Misjudging their friends

I've even gone on their Facebook pages and responded to their friends' posts. Okay, I've done that only once, but my son Ian sure hasn't forgotten it. I doubt he ever will.

A boy had been posting offensive remarks about people with disabilities on Ian's wall. (The kid thought he was being funny.) I'd seen that Ian had responded in what I thought was an appropriate way when this happened in the past, but one day when I was skimming over his page, I found another comment. I hated it being there, unchecked, tarnishing his wall like an obscene gesture.

I knew Ian wouldn't be home for hours to respond, so, impulsively, I logged out of my Facebook account, signed in as my son, and—masquerading as Ian—wrote under the boy's comment: "Dude, that was totally inappropriate!"

I thought I'd managed to sound *exactly* like my son.

When he arrived home, I confessed.

"You *what*? You posted on my wall? *As me*?"

"Um. Yes. I didn't like what that kid wrote."

"I don't either, but Mom, you said 'Dude'! And the way you use punctuation. That comma . . . I just can't believe you did that." He deleted my comment and posted his own, using neither the word *dude* nor *inappropriate*.

"Next time, let me handle it, okay?" Ian asked.

"I'm really sorry," I said. "It felt important at the moment. Can you forgive me?"

"Yeah. Well," he said. "Okay."

(Oops.)

Being a mom is a big job—a *mom*umental one, if you like mash-ups. Children are born with astonishing potential. As parents, we can create a home environment and develop relationships with our children that will stretch, ground, and prepare our children for lives of creativity, health, and love. Of course, our days as parents teem with everyday tasks related to our kids' physical, emotional, and intellectual needs. We cut fingernails, schedule dental appointments, keep our kids in clothes and shoes that fit them, monitor their homework and academic progress, give them hugs and kisses, encourage them in their spiritual lives, teach them manners, and do their laundry.

By the way, why doesn't anyone warn us that doing laundry will become something of a second career for us once we have kids? And, further, if they can put people on the moon and vehicles on Mars, why isn't there a machine that completes the entire process—from washing, to drying, to folding, to stacking clothes in our kids' drawers? *(Mr. Dyson? Anyone?)*

With that much, and more, on our plates, we're bound to mess up. All the parents whose dirty little secrets I've shared here—including me!—are loving moms and dads, *most of the time*. We are patient, *most of the time*. We model courtesy and respect for our children, *most of the time*. We are attentive, *most of the time*.

But sometimes we mess up. None of us is perfect, but I think my son was onto something when he said that what matters is what we do *most of the time*.

When we've actually done something wrong—shocked our child by tearing up his sticker, breaking her doll's neck, or sitting her down too hard on the steps for a time-out, we must take a breath, tell someone about it, apologize to the person we've wronged, and accept the grace that is always available to us from a loving God.

We have to start over, over, and over again in the funny, broken love that is family.

CHAPTER 4

Escape to Gordon's House
Adventures in Friendship

I closed the e-mail and sat back in my chair. My shoulders relaxed and I let out a breath that I'd been holding in, somehow, for weeks and weeks. I had just been given access to a magical escape hatch from the persistent cold, low light and mounds of gray snow that had narrowed the sightlines of my neighborhood for months. The e-mail was from a friend in Los Angeles saying she had been planning to redeem airline passes to fly to Chicago to visit me, but she quickly modified her thoughts after realizing that March where I live is hardly an ideal vacation destination.

In case you're wondering, the average high temperature we hardy Chicagoans muddle through in March is 45 degrees; the low is 28. I should note that, on average, we live with temperatures in the forties from about October to April. Those numbers translate to many fires in the fireplace, twice that many cups of hot chocolate, and plentiful cases of seasonal affective disorder.

"I was thinking. What if you used my passes and met me out here instead?" my friend suggested, likely wondering why on God's green earth I live where I do. "We could rent a house for the weekend. Maybe in Palm Springs."

The average high in Palm Springs, California, in March is over 80 degrees.

"You mean Chicago in late winter doesn't appeal to you?" I replied, teasing her.

"Meet me in the desert," she wrote. "And I'll see who else can make it out here."

I should note, in case you hadn't yet detected it, I'm a Midwestern girl. I like kicking through a blanket of fallen leaves in the woods and digging my hands into the pockets of my fleece jacket on a chilly day. I'm good at making fires in the fireplace, cooking with a slow cooker, and using the word *cozy* as a verb, as in "I'll cozy it up in here." It's not that I love relentlessly gray skies or that I don't appreciate the feel of warm sand under my feet, but most of my life, I've lived in the north.

I attempt—admittedly with only partial success—to "prefer the given," an idea my old professor Father McClatchy introduced to us in college. Coined by British author Charles Williams, the phrase means choosing to appreciate what we have instead of being dissatisfied with the grace and other gifts God gives us.

In other words, if winter is a northerner's lot in life for half of the year, what's the point in wishing it were otherwise?

A woman who lives near me attempts to "prefer the given" of winter by posting daily PWTs (positive weather thoughts) as her status updates on Facebook every day in colder months. Sometimes they are as simple as "Grateful that the sun is out today." Other times I can tell she is struggling to accept the day's weather. "At least the rain cleared away that dirty black ice on the sidewalk," she'll write. Or, "Lights on the bushes make dark afternoons a little brighter."

I'm a fan of the PWT and do try to prefer the given of winter, but—twist my arm!—I was willing to put more than sixteen hundred miles between myself and the sound of snowplows and salt trucks passing in the night.

I'd also just come through a challenging time. It wasn't so much the literal bleakness of the long winter that affected me, but I had been stuck in an in-between place that felt lonely and disheartening. Part of it was the strange letdown of having finished writing my first book. Writing it had been an emotional trek as I explored vulnerable memories. Shifting my focus back to my usual world of making lunches, shopping for groceries, and relating with the outside world felt strange and almost dreamlike. Although I'd completed those household tasks over the months, my gaze had been inward and otherwise occupied. I'd been going through the motions, ever writing and revising in my head. And months before its release, I had been initiated into the business of the administrative details and publicity tasks into which authors must plunge. I felt hollowed out.

These are First World problems, to be sure. My children were healthy, happy, and thriving. I had the peaceful home and functional marriage and family I'd longed for since I was a child. But I felt dragged down. A spiritual director to whom I'd gone for guidance told me she felt I had become "fractalized," or fragmented. She encouraged me to find quiet places to be with God, to try to do one thing at a time, and not to be so hard on myself. She told me she was praying that I would have eyes to see all the ways God was showing his love to me. Perhaps, in retrospect, part of my problem was that I was too burned out to see my life clearly, let alone "prefer" it. The Palm Springs trip was a gift and a sign of God's love for me. It felt like a clean break and an opportunity to recharge. I counted the weeks, then days, until it was time to go.

Finally the weekend came. Four friends and I traveled to Palm Springs from around the country. We left our children with our husbands, packed our swimsuits, and made our ways to the rental we would soon affectionately know as "Gordon's House."

After arriving in California, I went out to the curb, stood under a palm tree, and blinked in the warm, afternoon sun. A moment later my friend pulled up, jumped out of her car, and grabbed me in a hug.

"You can take your anorak off now," she said, tossing my bag into the back of her car.

Gordon's House was beautifully decorated and cleared of all its owner's personal effects, except one. On one of the bookshelves was a thin book that contained pictures taken at the house at a 1960s-themed birthday party. In miniskirts, leisure suits, wigs, and striking outrageous and comic poses, images of the aging guests at Gordon's party kept my friends and me laughing all weekend.

Gordon's House is a stellar example of Desert Modern architecture with an open floor plan, walls of windows, and a swimming pool. Beyond the pool in the backyard were two fruit trees, one orange and one grapefruit. Upon stepping into the yard, the gentle sunshine a kind of miracle, I walked to them, marveling at the palm trees and mountains that rose all around us. I reached up and plucked a grapefruit. Still standing under the tree, I tore into the fruit's thick peel and opened it.

Where was I?

Had I really stood in the freezing rain outside of O'Hare airport only hours before?

When we had all arrived from points east and west of Palm Springs, my friends and I sat together at a round, white lacquered table in the dining room. We gave each other gifts. Salted caramels. Beaded bracelets. Bath salts. A silver heart hung from a soft leather cord. No one bickered, asked for a ride to lacrosse practice, or needed to be told to use the potty. I didn't have to assign chores, answer a telephone, or check over homework. *It was bliss.* We were just five women, remembering what it was like just to take a deep breath and be ourselves. Our grown-up selves.

Looking around at my friends, I blurted out my first thought: "Even if we had to leave right now, this will have been the best weekend ever." The weekend, of course, didn't end then, but my exclamation became a catchphrase for us. As we cooked together, swam in the heated pool in the moonlight, or lounged on one of the huge sofas in the living room, one of us would exclaim, "Even if we had to leave right now . . ."

The weekend wasn't all about shopping or drinking pink martinis—activities that seem to be de rigueur when girls' weekends are portrayed on TV or in movies. In fact, none of us was interested in shopping for anything more than groceries. All of us are women who read, write, and edit professionally, and we had work to do. On Friday, we sat in companionable silence on deck chairs or at a glass table by the pool with our laptops. I occasionally went to the grapefruit tree to grab a snack. One friend set a gargantuan stack of magazine clips on the table in front of her, reading and critiquing them as she judged a writing contest. Another prepared lesson plans. Still another answered e-mail and worked through upcoming production schedules for her company. I wrote a few articles and blog posts, including a newspaper column on creativity in the digital age and a blog post about Charlie Sheen.[1] (Sheen, at the time, was the focus of the national spotlight for what turned out to be increasingly bizarre behavior.)

Our weekend at Gordon's House happened to be when a devastating earthquake hit Japan. One of us, Keiko, has family in that country and watched, grief-stricken, as the tragic news was delivered. For the rest of the night, we watched news coverage and sat around her like protective aunts, rubbing her back and praying for the safety of her family as she frantically tried to contact loved ones in Japan. Fortunately, thanks mostly to the power of Facebook, she was able to determine that her friends and family there were unharmed.

We five friends rarely talk on the phone. The majority of us, in fact, are allergic to that form of communication. But that weekend, between dozing in the sun, swimming, and tapping away on our laptops, we shared the private hopes and burdens that we'd not been able to articulate via e-mail. We thanked God together for our friendships and the other gifts he has given us. The two of us who'd come from the Midwest stood in the sun for long periods of time, our faces raised to the sky, soaking in the light. One friend, a brilliant woman whose life at this moment doesn't afford her much room to be the artist she is, said she felt like the four of us were midwives to her that weekend, helping to birth ideas that had been gestating in her, hidden away for so long.

We also talked about the way that motherhood changes us. Our girls' weekend didn't bring us back to who we were *before* we had children but invited us to explore and know who we are *now*. After all, who we were five or ten or fifteen years ago is sort of beside the point. All five of us are mothers. Two of us have children by adoption. Two have found what one has named "second-chance love" after losing first husbands, respectively, to cancer and to divorce. All of us continue to journey through our own losses, uncertainty, and pain. We spoke of the energy of girlhood and how we felt the tingling of that preteen buoyancy reappearing in our hearts and minds as we approached midlife.

"Even if we had to leave right now . . ."

On Sunday morning, we moved out of Gordon's House and went out for brunch before leaving for home. Azaleas hung off of trellises around our table. I looked from the faces of my friends to the brilliant pink flowers to the clear, sunny sky above and wondered if all of this would seem like a dream when I was home again that night.

(It would. It did.)

Amy Hilbrich Davis, the CEO and founder of Familylife success.com, encourages parents to maintain their friendships, even—or perhaps especially—during the most difficult seasons of parenthood. Moms and dads *need* friends, she reminds us.

"Friends play," Hilbrich Davis says. "They bring joy to your life. They make you laugh. Friends provide healthy perspective. They listen. Friends save you when you're sinking. They remind you of your priorities. Friends are life-sustaining. They are invaluable."[2]

"You know something I love about you?" my daughter Isabel asked me recently as we sat on the couch, my arm pulled around her.

"Tell me!"

"I like your friends," she said. She snuggled in close and looked into my eyes. "They make you happy, and they make me happy too."

We *do* need friends. Real friends. We need people to whom we can say our worst things on our worst days, particularly when children are very small and our worlds, similarly, seem to shrink too. We need heart friends who accept us as we are, see the best in us, and are comforting presences to us wherever we are in life.

"The best advice I ever gave to a friend when she was a new mom is that there are days when you really think you can't stand it *one more moment*," a woman tells me. "The baby won't stop crying. You're so lonely and isolated. Everything's messy. Everything smells bad. Terrible thoughts enter your mind. To leave your family. To abandon the baby. Or something even worse. But just telling someone how desperate you feel releases you from those kinds of thoughts. If it's a friend who has gone through it before, sometimes you can even find a way to laugh about it."

Getting away for a few days works wonders too, as I found at Gordon's House and during many other times in the course of my parenting. Although, for most of us, most of the time, a trip to an exotic locale is out of reach, there are other ways to get a break. Had my children been a few years younger than they were, I doubt I would have been able to take the time for the getaway to Palm Springs. But at this moment in life, it was possible to accept the gift of the airline passes and pack my bags.

When my children were much younger, my husband made extended business trips. He still travels for work, but a flagging economy reduced the number of times he's sent abroad every year and shortened the trips' duration. (Silver linings, I suppose.) Although I might be remembering this detail incorrectly, it seemed that *all* of his longer trips needed to be taken in the winter when, as previously established, the warmest it got for months at a time was not so warm at all.

The combination of winter, four children, and single, stay-at-home parenting was a recipe for cabin fever of the most extreme sort. Every week was a blur of numbers and household tasks for me. One hundred nails to trim. Five sets of teeth, twice a day, either to brush or to oversee their brushing. Forty library books to check out, read, and return. One hundred twenty-six meals to prepare. Eighty-four socks to wash, dry, and pair. Countless scraped elbows and knees to bandage.

Sometimes, regardless of whether they were a few days or weeks, my husband's trips never seemed to end. When my kids were too young to read the clocks, I took to misrepresenting the time. Remember what I said earlier: desperate times call for desperate measures. Anyway, the extra sleep was good for them. Having four overtired kids and a husband half a world away is no fun for anyone.

"Oops. Almost bedtime! Time for tubs!" I'd announce at about five-thirty or six instead of the usual seven o'clock. Sunsets in the late afternoon were my accomplice in this ruse. After getting the children bathed, read to, prayed with, and safely tucked into bed, I'd busy myself loading up the preschool backpacks with sneakers, empty paper towel rolls, a canned food item that starts with *T*, or whatever was the requested item on the half sheet of paper from their teachers. I'd then crawl under the kitchen table to chip away at the dried spackle of rice cereal, yogurt, and pasta that coated the floorboards. I'd load the dishwasher, check on whichever child was calling for me, pick up toys, and then retreat to the basement to attack the principal job of the evening: the laundry.

(Isn't being a mommy glamorous?)

Most of the time, I failed to put smaller numbers, numbers that related to my own care and well-being, on the daily to-do list. What I aspired for every day was to spend thirty minutes on the treadmill, take one hot bath at the end of the day, and read for one hour before going to sleep. On the rare occasions I accomplished even one of those tasks, I was a more balanced person and more equipped to mother the following day. But it was rare that I did.

Self-care continues to elude me too much of the time, even now that my kids are older. After the kids are off to school, I open the kitchen cabinet to put away the cinnamon sugar and find myself taking all of the spices out onto the counter, washing down the shelves, checking expiration dates, and tossing out old jars. As I close the cabinet, I notice that someone has spilled grape juice and it's splattered and dried on the wall. I wash it, noticing that the baseboards are in dire need of washing. After crouching down and moving around the room spraying and cleaning, I glance over at the clock on the microwave and see that it's way past when I was supposed to start my workday and I decide that, yet again, I must forego jogging on the treadmill. (Alas.)

But when they were very young and David was traveling for work, I almost always failed to take good care of myself. I think of it now, every time I'm sitting on a plane and the flight attendants do their safety spiel. They inform passengers that, in case of loss of cabin pressure, oxygen masks will drop from the ceiling. They instruct us to pull our masks toward ourselves and position them over our noses and mouths. Only after securing the elastic band behind our heads are we directed to assist any small children beside us. The message is clear—we'll be no help to our children if we're unconscious and slumped over in our seats. Too many parents, in the thick of caring for little ones, have reversed those steps—even after securing the oxygen masks for our children, we forget to put on our own.

During those periods of single-parenthood, I tried to prefer the given. Winter could be snow angels and marshmallows and hot chocolate, right? Of course it was, but in reality, it also could mean chapped lips, hacking coughs, and drooping heaps of wet snow pants. Many days, I lit a fire in the fireplace, piled pillows and blankets in front of it, and read to the children. I bought a giant roll of craft paper and we did art projects at the kitchen table. After the excruciatingly long bundle-up period, we all went outside and played in the snow until someone lost a mitten or the sky grew too dark to see.

Not long ago, while looking through some old pictures, my daughter pointed out that our snowmen sported red, green, and blue polka dots.

"Why did our snowmen look like that?" Isabel asked. "With those funny dots?"

"One of you insisted on it," I answered. "I can't remember whose idea it was. Somehow it was very important to that person that our snow people didn't look like everyone else's. So I let you use food coloring."

"They're weird," Isabel said.

"Yeah, I guess they are."

While David was away, I was grateful for each and every minute in which the kids were happily occupied. I remembered those long days and how happy I'd been when the polka dot project began. Letting them all squeeze colors onto the snowmen busied the children for an extra half hour each time we did it. After our outside adventures, we'd all trudge back inside, again. I made hot chocolate, again. I arranged mittens, gloves, and hats over the heat registers, again. I hung the snow pants and coats to dry in the laundry room, again.

Meanwhile, David was across the globe working in India. On longer business trips, the kids would sometimes say to me, "I can't remember what Daddy looks like anymore." (I didn't share that tidbit with him. He already missed them terribly.) Although his longest trip approached three weeks, most were shorter.

My friend Elizabeth's husband also traveled for work. Our sons were friends and, back then, we had a secret agreement that when one of our children was invited to a birthday party that for whatever reason we didn't want them to attend, we could use the other family as an excuse. We knew it would have taken our boys weeks to recover had we allowed them to go to some of the extravagant and overstimulating parties to which they were invited.

We were each other's built-in excuse, free pass, and "Get Out of Jail Free" card.

"Oh, I'm sorry, honey," one of us might tell our four, year-old son. "But you aren't free for the combination paintball, Chuck E. Cheese, laser-tag sleepover next Friday. We're getting together with . . ."

And we would plan an outing together.

Once, when both of our husbands were traveling, I called Elizabeth.

"Would you and the boys like to have a sleepover on Friday? I think I'm sort of losing it here," I said. "Bring them in their pajamas. They can all sleep in the basement in sleeping bags. And our living room couch folds out. You could sleep by the fire."

She accepted my offer in a heartbeat.

"It would be nice to have a little adult company," I murmured, trying not to sound desperate.

That winter night we *talked*. I couldn't believe what it was like to speak to an adult again and to laugh about something more nuanced than the antics of Bob the Builder or Elmo and his goldfish, Dorothy. The bigger kids played games, watched a movie, and slept on sleeping bags in the basement. They were happily occupied with the novelty of it all. My friend and I sat by the fire and laughed.

When Elizabeth and her boys left the next morning, I was restored. I found myself paying better attention to my children and being able to appreciate the ordinary blessings around me.

A little hand reaching up to hold mine.
A drawing of a row of hearts on a roll of craft paper.
The smiles on my children's faces.
A polka-dotted snowman.

Signs You Might Be Burned Out
and in Need of a Getaway with Friends

☐ You can't remember your favorite color.
☐ You can't think of the last time you laughed until you snorted.
☐ You remind your colleague to "use the potty" before the meeting begins.
☐ You no longer fantasize about a vacation to Hawaii, but instead daydream about getting nine uninterrupted hours of sleep.
☐ You weep over everything from a chipped mug to an episode of *Dinosaur Train*.
☐ You can't complete tasks that you once considered simple, such as unloading the dishwasher, putting in a pair of earrings, or spooning the cottage cheese into a bowl before consuming it.
☐ Your heart sinks every time the phone rings.
☐ You make up excuses not to go out in public—to church, to school functions, or even to the end of the driveway to bring in the trashcans.
☐ You think things that feel too shameful to share. These can include, but are not limited to, imagining a romantic tryst between you and your child's pediatrician, taking your baby to a grocery store and leaving her in the cart, and telling your boss what you really think of your job.

Scoring:

- If you checked **1–2 boxes,** consider yourself fortunate. Keep investing in healthy friendships that make you *glad* to be you. Send your true friends a note in the mail—yes, the real mail—to tell them how much you appreciate them. (Consider suggesting that you all meet for a weekend in Palm Springs.)

- If you checked **3–4 boxes,** acknowledge that you are headed toward Mommy Burnout. (See appendix 2.) Tell someone how you are feeling. Find ways to be restored: create a playgroup with trusted neighbors and friends, join a MOPS (Mothers of Preschoolers) group (www.mops.org), or trade babysitting hours with a friend. (Also, do a little research on rentals in Palm Springs.)

- If you checked **5+ boxes,** do all of the tasks listed for **3–4** checkmarks and, additionally, speak to a therapist, doctor, pastor, and/or other trusted person about how exhausted and out of sorts you are. It's time to get help. (And get to Palm Springs at your earliest convenience: *360 days of sun! Joshua Tree National Park! Orange trees!*)

CHAPTER 5

Behind the Amish
Adventures in the Basics

On an August morning a few summers ago, just as the sun was coming up, my family and I began the thirteen-hour drive from the suburbs of Chicago to South Dakota's Black Hills. By noon, we were in Minnesota, not yet setting sail on that massive ocean of land that is South Dakota. My children are familiar with—or you might say desensitized to—the adversities that long car trips demand: having to "hold it" until a rest stop is located, scrunched and restless legs, the tedium of hour after hour (especially because their countercultural parents refused to allow DVD or videoplayers in the car), and one sibling or another reclining their seat too far back or migrating past an agreed-upon boundary line. All of these issues take their toll on children during car rides of more than a dozen hours.

You might have already guessed that those exotic journeys I dreamed of as a girl haven't quite materialized for my family of six. We aren't packing steamer trunks for a trip down the Nile or buying climbing gear for a trek to Mount Everest. Instead, the night before our decidedly domestic vacations, my husband and I put the kids into bed in their sweats and load up the van with pillows and books on tape and a cooler full of cheese sticks, fruit, and juice boxes. I make goody bags full of treats and distractions for each child—books, PEZ dispensers, and art supplies—and leave them on their assigned seats. The next morning before sunrise, David and I pull the kids out of bed, shuffle them into the car, and begin the long drive to end points such as Savannah, Boston, or—in this case—Rapid City. I start to doze off before we're out of the county, the sound of PEZ dispensers clicking away behind me in the backseats.

As we barreled along Route 90 toward Sioux City that August day, I told my husband I was ready to take my turn driving, but first I needed a cup of coffee. Good coffee. Real coffee. I was not willing, I clarified, to accept a polystyrene cup of swill that had been sitting too long on a gas station hot plate. David was just beginning to protest that I didn't need to be quite so particular about coffee on road trips when a sign caught my eye. Although I'd seen dozens of them that day, this sign—in contrast to those that trumpeted the imminent approach of a Burger

King or truckstop diner—seemed somehow lit from above, as though a celestial spotlight was shining down on it. It felt like an answer, a gift. On a big brown star I read the words: Cabin Coffee Co.

"That's it," I told David. "Get off at the next exit."

We found Cabin Coffee in St. Charles, Minnesota—a town whose population is fewer than four thousand. It's a bit of a drive off the interstate, but I insisted to my time-conscious husband that we must make the effort to get there. After all, I'd seen a *sign*. We drove past an auto parts store, someone's deserted yard sale, and scattered antique stores, realty offices, and other small businesses.

"How far is this place?" my husband moaned.

As we pulled deeper into St. Charles, we were further delayed when an Amish couple riding on a horse cart approached the intersection a few blocks ahead and then turned in front of us.

"Oh great," David said darkly. "First you've got to have fancy coffee and now we've got the flipping Amish in front of us. We're *never* going to get there."

"David!" I scolded. "*Really!*"

David was in an uncharacteristically surly mood. He had been up late packing the car the night before, had woken up before four that morning, and was stressed about getting us to South Dakota in time to meet friends. For the record, he is of good, Pennsylvania Mennonite stock and usually exhibits nothing but respect for the Amish.

At their father's outburst, the kids sat up and looked

out the front of the car. It was their first time seeing Amish people up close, the husband in his straw hat and beard, the wife in her bonnet and simple dress.

"What's with *those two*?" Theo asked.

"The flipping Amish," Ian repeated, delighted with the phrase.

The kids erupted into raucous laughter, pointing at the two people primly riding their cart in front of us. I tried to bring them all to order. In my most sensible voice, I decided to give a lesson on the Amish in America. My need for caffeine, however, and the early hour of our departure rendered me incapable of thinking of how to describe this culture to my kids.

"Yes, they're Amish," I said. "They're, um, Christians. And very peaceful."

"Peaceful. No kidding!" Theo said. "Clippety-clop. Clippety-clop."

The children were overcome by fits of giggles.

"What's with the clothes?" Ian shouted.

"And the wagon!" Isabel said.

"They live simply," I said.

"You *think*?" Theo said, his voice brimming in sarcasm.

"They don't use electricity—" Here I was interrupted by gales of laughter from the back of the car.

"No lights? How do they see?" Mia asked.

"You know, they use sunlight in the daytime. And then . . . well, candles, I guess," I said, beginning to giggle in spite of myself. "They live at a much slower pace."

"Slower pace, all right," David grumbled. "I can't get around them."

"Flipping Amish," Theo said, in solidarity with his father.

Then we saw it—a pristine log cabin that looked to be plunked down in the middle of a new black parking lot. *Cabin Coffee Co.* Our Amish friends continued down the road as David hit the gas pedal and veered a little too quickly, in my humble opinion, into the parking lot. He parked the car, grabbed the leash, and stormed off to walk the dog in a vacant lot nearby.

"Everyone go to the bathroom here," he ordered, calling over his shoulder. "Twice if possible. We're not stopping again until dinner."

"Yep. I'll go twice," Ian giggled. "Maybe even three times."

The kids and I made our way into the coffee shop, punchy and unkempt after so many hours in the car. They were still whispering to each other about the Amish couple, giggling over the unfamiliar sight.

Cabin Coffee Co. had a playful, Western theme and a friendly air about it. Its company slogan, "Just be happy . . . and have fun!" called to us from signs, T-shirts, and coffee mugs.

Isabel pointed to a mug. "That should be our new family motto!" she said.

"Great idea! I love it," I said. "All in favor?"

The five of us raised our hands.

"All opposed?"

No one moved; the motion was passed.

I ordered a latte, fruit smoothies, and bagel sandwiches. The girl behind the counter chatted with me, smiling affectionately at my gaggle of children. My kids shuffled in and out of the restroom and then dropped one by one onto the wood-framed sofas and looked contently around the store.

"The bathroom's actually *clean*," Theo whispered to me, aware that his mother has just the teeny-tiniest case of germophobia. (By "teeny-tiniest," I mean that it's actually a bit of a problem. You should see the drawer in my kitchen that is stocked with individual handy wipes and small bottles of hand sanitizer.)

"And you'll like what they painted on the walls," Theo added.

Along the top of the restroom walls was hand-painted, in whimsical text, "Love. Joy. Peace. Patience. Kindness. Goodness. Faithfulness. Gentleness. Self-control." The fruit of the Spirit.

Everything seemed right in the world.

Back on the highway, the squall of crabbiness, sarcasm, and mockery had blown over. The gas tank was full. David had fallen asleep in a flash, his pillow crushed against the window. I cradled my latte in my hand and clicked on the cruise control and the stereo. My daughters had sketch pads spread out on their laps and were drawing the "Just be happy . . . and have fun" logo with their markers. The boys pulled chunks of strawberries from their smoothies. The dog was stretched out on the floor. I felt like I was swimming in a pool full of gratitude as we passed the green hills and farms of Minnesota with Van Morrison crooning about fields of wonder and a bridge where angels dwell.

Thank you, God, I prayed.

That stop in Minnesota is the kind of experience my friend Cathleen Falsani describes in her book *Sin Boldly: A Field Guide for Grace*.[1] In each of the book's chapters, Falsani finds God's presence and, yes, gift of grace in what may at first glance seem like unlikely places. A preacher on late-night TV. A Kenyan slum. The grocery store. When she talks about grace, Falsani waves away theological arguments over whether one kind of grace (common? divine?) is superior to another.

Common grace, by the way, is understood as God's provision to all people and can refer to anything from medical advancements that benefit humanity to the sun rising every morning to—yes—the discovery of an idyllic, perfectly placed coffee shop on the prairie. Divine grace, theologians explain, is the love and mercy of a God who became incarnate to bring redemption to humankind.

But both types of grace are outpourings of God's love for us, and Falsani writes that splitting hairs as we define different types of grace is "like bickering about what color God's eyes are."

She then adds, "They're hazel, in case you were wondering."[2] (I love that.)

Family life affords us countless opportunities to receive and dispense grace. Grace is the way our kids forgive us after we lose our tempers. Grace is a baby's fever breaking after a long, frightening night. Grace is sprouted marigold seeds in a Styrofoam cupful of dirt. Grace is building sandcastles, playing soccer in the backyard, and dancing with our kids. Grace is seeing a child bloom in adolescence, the beauty and strength of his adult self shining through.

Too often when we travel at the speed of modern family life, we're in a blur. We fail to slow down, take a breath, and see God's grace all around us. Maybe modern families would do well to clip-clop along like our Amish friends once in a while instead of strapping ourselves in, tucking in our ear buds, and keeping our eyes glued onto brightly lit screens as real life flies by us.

The simplicity of Amish life is attractive to a fast-paced culture that's on information overload. That longing to slow down and experience grace—both common and divine—might explain why any novel whose cover features a woman wearing a bonnet seems destined for the bestseller lists these days. We wonder what would it be like to live without the constant distractions of advertisements, ringing cell phones, and e-mail notifications.

For one thing, I bet our children would be less stressed than they are.

After all, if my kids would be done with school once and for all after eighth grade like the Amish, I doubt I'd give their report cards a second thought. If they had guaranteed jobs on the farm or in the woodwork shop, I'd never worry about their future in what is an unpredictable—or predictably dreary—economy. If I knew that their identities were simply to "be Amish," I wouldn't spend so much mental energy puzzling through how much time and money to invest in music lessons, sports, or other pursuits that might shape who my children are and bring them satisfaction in later life.

But, having said all of that, I don't envy the Amish. I like our lives "out here." I like the color, vibrancy, and commotion a diverse world affords. I like going to movies, attending concerts, and otherwise seeing what my culture is saying about what it means to be a human being right now. And I *really, really* like being able to press a button to let a machine clean the clothes or wash the dishes. (Don't get me started about my robot vacuum. Let's just say it was love at first sight.)

A few years ago, one hundred children's authors, teachers, and other experts on childhood wrote an open letter to the *Daily Telegraph* newspaper in the United Kingdom, expressing their concern about how modern society is "misshaping" and even killing childhood.[3] The group included children's author Philip Pullman and child development expert Penelope Leach. They asserted that our culture has changed too much and childhood has become too complex in recent years. One writer said what is poisoning childhood is "a sinister cocktail of junk food, marketing, overcompetitive schooling and electronic entertainment."[4] The result? An epidemic of pediatric anxiety and depression.

"[Children] still need what developing human beings have always needed, including real food (as opposed to processed 'junk'), real play (as opposed to sedentary, screen-based entertainment), first-hand experience of the world they live in and regular interaction with the real-life significant adults in their lives," the letter said.[5]

(I imagine Amish children *do* have all of those things.)

Reading that letter reminded me, deep into the parenting of my children, of some of the essential components of raising a healthy family. Real food. Real play. Real interaction with adults. Without those things, the letter writers assert, children suffer. Countless physicians and researchers agree. And more and more kids *are* suffering; stress and depression among children are on the rise.[6]

When we wax eloquent about childhood, we describe it as a happy, peaceful time. There are few demands on children as they ride their bikes around the neighborhood, stare at ant trails on the sidewalk, and get lost in their daydreams. These kinds of childhood pastimes, however, are fading. We've gone way past "the right kind of busy"—whatever in the world that could mean—into a spinning world where children are closely managed, overscheduled, and lacking time and space for free play.

And play matters.

In an article in the *Atlantic* titled "All Work and No Play: Why Your Kids Are More Anxious, Depressed," pediatrician Esther Entin asserts that there are lifelong, detrimental consequences to children having too little free playtime. She writes, "When parents realize the major role that free play can take in the development of emotionally healthy children and adults, they may wish to reassess [their] priorities." She suggests that parents "back off" from scheduling so many supervised activities, hover less, and let the kids roam a bit in "free, imaginative, kid-directed play."[7]

When I think of my interactions with my kids, I see myself too often holding a pad of sticky notes in my hand, jotting down a chore list. Or checking their homework assignments and grades online. Or reminding them to put away their shoes, empty their backpacks, or fill the dog's water bowl. Managing a houseful of kids, taking care of a dog, and being—as is true for most of the women I know—the coordinator of medical appointments, menu planning, social gatherings, and myriad other details for a family of six requires strategic organization.

And I've gotten quite organized over the years. I have an inbox for school papers, permission slips, and birthday invitations. The kids have regular chores. Every morning—thanks to instructions I learned years ago from Fly Lady[8]—I have a routine that I think of as "the sweep through." I jog through each room of the house, starting in the kids' bedrooms. I pick up stray socks and dirty clothes and put them down the laundry chute. I wipe down bathroom counters. I make sure there are bars of soap, shampoo in the bottles, and rolls of toilet paper where needed. I start a load of laundry, plan what we'll have for dinner, and then get to the work that results in a paycheck. Once I know the house is set for the day, I can focus.

I must confess, though, that as I think strategically about the home I'm creating and the children I'm raising, I rarely give thought to how much "free play" time each child is getting.

Fortunately, they seem to work that bit out for themselves. Maybe what I can do as a parent is leave space in my children's schedules, as much as possible, for them to get bored. When they're "bored," my kids hop the fence and play lacrosse or soccer at a nearby college football field with their friends. They shoot funny videos with their cell phones. They construct forts and complicated Rube Goldberg machines with the wooden blocks, dominoes, and train sets of their earlier childhoods. They play baseball games in the backyard, with trees and the play set assigned the roles of first, second, and third base. They still love grabbing flashlights, whatever the season, and playing Ghost in the Graveyard outside at night. The younger ones spin themselves into a dizzy stupor playing a game called Texas Star Gazing, staring up at the sky while twirling around.

They do these things when nothing else is on the calendar, and when they have the chance to get a little bored and restless.

I try to ignore the gargantuan corn on the cob, molded in plastic, that floats above my head. As I stand in line at Target, I can almost feel it stirring up there, threatening to drop from the wires that suspend it from the ceiling. I take a few steps forward to get out from under it and then notice the enormous sunglasses—as big as a kayak—that hang from the ceiling twenty yards from the corn. Their presence shouts to me that, despite the recent cold weather and storms, summer is actually here.

Are these decorations meant to deliver panic attacks to customers? (Or is that just me?)

I have nothing against the season. I like knowing I have a break from packing lunches and unpacking backpacks. I like the sound of a Cubs game on the radio and the buzz of a lawnmower and the warble of the ice cream truck as it winds around town, playing tunes as crazily varied as "Oh Come All Ye Faithful" and "The Entertainer."

But summer's been less about Popsicles and the smell of freshly mown grass for me the last few years. Now that my kids are older and I've become a full-fledged "working mom," it's been more about driving them to activities, co-ordinating babysitters, and trying to squeeze in hours of work while still seeming accessible and like I'm home. (By the way, that smell wafting in from the grill is charbroiled guilt.)

The other day, my youngest asked my husband, "When's *your* last day, Dad?"

When he explained that he doesn't get the summer off, she frowned. I noted that it didn't occur to her to ask me the same question. As a work-from-home parent, I'm always here, more or less.

Carla Barnhill has written on her blog about creating happy summers for ourselves as well as for our children. "I am trying to keep our calendar low on plans and high on free time," Barnhill says. "That has meant a lot of saying no, something that doesn't come naturally for me but that I find to be terrifically rewarding."[9]

Barnhill says no to camps or lessons that span over more than a week and activities that require most of the family to be observers, such as one child's baseball games. She also keeps one day a week completely free of commitments. Her good ideas inspired me to come up with some summer strategies of my own. As much as possible, I register my kids for activities they can do *together*. I make a summer schedule of working hours and force myself to clock out each day when the kids tromp in from camps, caddying, or when the babysitter's allotted hours are done.

I want to be intentional about being present with them.

In her blog post, Barnhill also addresses the dreaded "I'm bored" proclamation that too often emerges from our children's lips over the course of summer. She writes, "Boredom is a kid's best friend . . . there is research that suggests that the brain needs downtime to process information and cast a vision for the future. . . . Nothing gives the brain space and time like boredom. . . . This isn't a problem that needs a solution."[10]

As a semiprofessional daydreamer, I absolutely agree with her about boredom. I've decided that when one of my four kids says she or he is "bored," I will respond by reciting something the great Indian sculptor Anish Kapoor has said: "It's precisely in those moments when I don't know what to do, boredom drives one to try . . . a host of possibilities . . . [to] either get somewhere or not get anywhere."[11]

I printed several copies of that quote and issue them, like a combination traffic ticket/gift certificate, to my kids when they utter the dreaded *b* word.

Who knows? Maybe in that moment of not knowing what to do, the kids will be inspired to go to the library and conduct a little research. Maybe they'll even learn about Anish Kapoor, or the Amish.

Summer break and family vacations, of course, afford the most time for boredom and free play. The kids roam, explore, and invent. On our vacations to South Dakota with our friends Mark and Mary and their girls, the kids disappear for most of the day. In the morning, they spring from our cabins and make themselves scarce with their unofficial cousins until the ringing of a brass bell draws them for meals. They pretend to be pirates in the forest. (Fallen tree trunks make ships, and black eye patches are easily procured from the drugstore in town.) They invent complex games involving squirt guns and jumping, cannonball-style, into the pool. They play roller-blade basketball. The bigger ones climb up the side of a mountain and scamper up rock walls—yes, all by themselves. And no, they've never fallen down a cliff.

(Not yet, anyway.) We parents sneak them out of bed at night to lie on picnic tables and stare at the stars. When they scrape their knees or get splinters, they appear out of the woods, but after a quick first-aid pit stop, they are off again. Admittedly, these trips are not comparable to visiting the Great Wall of China or the Pantheon, but our summer vacations are a source of grace—and play—for all of us.

The evening after we discovered Cabin Coffee Co., despite the unplanned stop in Minnesota and being slowed down by the Amish, we made it on time to meet our friends in South Dakota. On arrival, we traded our crumpled clothes for swimming suits and jumped in the pool. Later, as we unpacked our cars, we told stories of the road.

"Dad was crabby," Isabel said, tattling on her father.

"He almost ran over this Amish family," Ian said.

David apologized for being gruff toward his Anabaptist brother and sister, and he was forgiven.

We told our friends the story of the perfect coffee shop, the slow-moving horse cart, and our new family motto. *Just be happy . . . and have fun.* Maybe in parenting, much like making a cross-country trip, the key is to begin with the destination in mind. If we want to raise whole, confident adults, we need to remember that they need what is real. Real food. Real play. Real interactions with others. And while making that journey, with its necessary—and unnecessary—detours and moments of boredom, we need to keep our eyes open for moments of real grace.

Whether or not we're Amish.

CHAPTER 6

There's Something about Blue French Fries
Adventures in Junk Culture

More than a decade ago, a few weeks before Christmas, my friend Mary and I were shopping with my two sons. Ian was one year old and buckled into his stroller. Theo was three and stood on a built-in step riding behind his brother. Mary and I were walking the aisles of an electronics store looking for presents for our husbands. The two of us were in a silly, festive mood, examining electric windshield deicers and white noise machines. I parked the stroller as Mary and I played with a pair of yellow walkie-talkies. Calling each other "Bandit" and "Cledus," we mimicked the old trucker movie *Smokey and the Bandit*.

"Breaker-breaker, you read me?" I said. (Of course she

did. Although the walkie-talkies had no batteries, we were standing right next to each other.)

"Loud and clear," Mary said.

"Cledus, I'll catch you in Texarkana."

"I read you, Bandit," she said, using her best drawl. (Mary's from Arkansas; she can do a good Cledus.)

After a moment, we put the handsets down and glanced at my boys. They were staring at a television. On the screen, a corporate spokesperson demonstrated how a particular mattress could be soft on one side of the bed and firm on the other. I started to push the stroller away.

"Wait—wait! It's not over," Theo protested.

"Well, how about that, Jen?" Mary said, teasing me. "You've got him watching *product demos*. You sure that's better than *Playhouse Disney*?"

"That's a big ten-four, Cledus," I said.

Months before, when I told her why I'd booted TV from my home, Mary had been amused (and slightly puzzled) by the story. My decision to do so had come about dramatically during a time when David and I were deeply immersed in that twilight zone that is the world of raising small children. With two young sons and a baby on the way, David and I were overtired, understimulated, and not sure when—or if—we would ever feel like ourselves again. In the evenings, it was rare that we did anything except bathe the boys and get them to sleep, tidy up the house, and fall into bed ourselves.

"When did you say their parents were coming to pick

them up?" David would ask me wearily, attempting a dark joke.

Sometimes when the boys were down for the night, we would try to have a conversation. This usually involved David staring out the window into the night, exhausted and consumed by his new career in software, while I stared at his reflection in the window and discussed the minutiae of my day at home. I'd tell him how this one might be constipated or that one had learned a new word. I'd share observations I'd made about the neighbors. One woman ironed every night at eleven. Across the street, the neighbors were putting in a new fence. Maybe they were getting a dog, I speculated. And then there were the reports of what I'd done all day with the kids.

Even I would find myself bored by some of the anecdotes I shared with him.

"So then I told him not to be so frustrated," I'd report. "He'd already built a big castle out of the blocks. It was good, actually. The castle, I mean. Well, the drawbridge wasn't really attached, but that's very hard to do, don't you think? He was so proud of what he'd made, though. It was fun to see. David? *David*? Are you with me?"

"What? Yeah. The drawbridge. Drawbridges are hard," David would murmur.

Often, we'd forego the scintillating conversation when our chores were done and just turn on the TV.

In those days making the effort to go out in the evening even just to rent a video—yes, on VHS—and spend the evening watching it was a significant event. It meant much more than just forfeiting the tête-à-têtes about spit-up or the contents of our son's diaper, but required that we sacrifice at least ninety minutes of sleep. This was no small matter.

The movie David had rented one fateful night was *There's Something about Mary*. Released in 1998, it was an enormous box-office success. I doubt we could have missed that it was billed as a "gross-out romantic comedy," but we were likely in the market for a good laugh and thought the movie would provide us with a temporary escape from what was often a grueling time in our lives.

But seeing it that night—or the portion of it that I watched, anyway—changed our family life forever. The movie was so full of . . . um . . . inappropriate situations and, mostly, was so very *not* entertaining to me that I not only grabbed the television cord and yanked the plug out from the wall, but also decided to rethink my relationship with American culture. Now before you start throwing stones and calling me a prude, I need to confess that I have many times before and since that evening laughed at bawdy, silly comedies. Trust me, no one who knows me even marginally would call my tastes puritanical. And, yes, I've already been told by several friends that they think the movie is hilarious.

But that night, about a half hour into *There's Something about Mary*, I stood up from the sofa.

"That's *it*!" I shouted. "I have *had it*!"

Looking back, I realize it wasn't just that particular

movie that sent me over the edge, but all of the useless junk that I felt my culture was selling to me.

Years before, when I moved to New York City after having grown up in the Midwest, I brought my unfailing politeness with me. Numerous times a day, I'd pass men—it was always men—holding out colored fliers advertising everything from restaurant specials to concerts in the Bowery to "girlie shows." As I passed each person and his fliers, he'd reach toward me and I would graciously accept the piece of paper.

"Thank you," I said, cheerfully, making eye contact with the person who had given me the paper whenever possible.

Sitting on the subway on the way home from work, I'd pull folded and crumpled papers from my coat pockets or briefcase and page through them. Inevitably, on exiting the train, I'd toss the whole lot into a garbage can on the platform. There was nothing worth keeping, no information I wanted, and in fact sometimes my eyes had scanned images and words I'd rather not have seen. After a few weeks in New York, I stopped reaching out and taking colored fliers from the guys on the sidewalk.

Incidentally, at about the same time, I also stopped giving whatever loose change I had in my pockets to anyone who asked for it. Admittedly, I can be a slow learner about such things, but on the fourth day in a row that the very same woman stopped me on the platform at Lexington

Avenue and told me it was her first day of work and she had dropped her wallet on the train and just needed a few dollars to get to her job, I got wise. My feelings were also a bit hurt that she didn't remember me from the previous few days. I felt like we'd started to get to know one other.

So, watching *There's Something about Mary*, and irritated beyond measure, I felt the same way I did in New York City those years ago. I wondered why I kept stuffing my pockets and my mind with useless and offensive junk. I wondered why I kept giving away my money to people who were lying to me.

Now, I'll admit to overthinking certain things from time to time and being perhaps just the littlest bit neurotic, but even in those early, sleep-deprived years in parenting, my hunch was right that my culture was changing. Further, I was worried about the way it would affect my children's minds and hearts as they grew. Companies had begun aggressively marketing to children on television in ways that they didn't when I was a child. Childhood, as author and sociology professor Juliet Schor so eloquently describes, had been "commodified."[1] Schor writes, "In the early days of children's marketing, most of the people who made commercials or crafted branding strategies relied on personal experience. They were parents and considered their own children to be good representations of the target audience. Today, most of the how-to books on children's marketing explicitly condemn such an approach. . . . Instead, they counsel, extensive research is necessary to succeed."[2]

One item that was likely developed after such careful research was Ore-Ida's Funky Fries. (Remember those?) The company knew kids loved french fries, bright colors, and fun food, so they came out with a new line that combined all three! Yippee! One flavor of french fries was chocolate and another was cinnamon. And then there were the "Kool Blue" fries that were as blue as a can of bright blue Play-Doh or, say, a barrel of toxic waste. For those who look with concern at the rise of pediatric health issues, the connection between ADHD and chemicals, sugar, and food dye made Funky Fries a particularly bad choice for kids.[3] The amount of trans fat in the fries was nothing to brag about either. The blue fries were just one example of junk products made for and marketed to children that would provide no real nutrition or other benefit to them— and indeed could harm their health. Happily, wise parents everywhere decided that feeding their kids blue french fries was going too far. The product flopped after about a year. (Blue fries. *Really*.)

On the *There's Something about Mary* night, I had a moment of clarity and saw that too much of my culture was built around the relentless quest for every kind of fleeting pleasure without regard to its consequences. It seemed to me that junk TV, crude and humorless movies, and so much else about our society was just a distraction. The underlying message—that pleasure should be our only and truest goal—flashed its face to me that night. It was ugly and sinister.

"I have had it," I said to David again. "And I want my time back. I wish I'd been doing anything else than watching that tonight. I don't want the TV. *At all. Anymore.*"

As I mentioned previously, TV and I would get back together later, but with new rules and expectations about the relationship. (Obviously, we weren't the only ones to draw new boundaries; savvy parents today routinely skip over commercials using new technology that is only a click away on their remotes.)

"We don't have to finish watching the movie," David offered. I don't recall now whether he had been enjoying the movie, but I'm sure he could tell I was serious about making a significant change. He also knew that when I was pregnant, I was not a person to be crossed.

"I'm sick of it. There's just so much garbage I can put up with and I have had it."

"But what about *ER*?" he asked, meekly. We'd watched that show together for years.

"I can live without it."

"*Seinfeld*?"

I shook my head.

"Or . . ." I could tell he was reaching, trying hard to keep my decision from hardening and getting set in stone. "Well, what about that cute English show you like? With those people who have the chickens. Or maybe goats. I mean, they farm in their backyard."

"*Good Neighbors*. I don't care," I said. He'd never called it "cute" before; I could tell he was working hard.

"Bill Nye the Science Guy?" he yelped in one last-ditch effort to change my mind.

"I can check him out from the library."

Before *There's Something about Mary* pulled me up from the comfort of my family room couch, I was a champion channel surfer. And, as I pounded through the channels, I glimpsed scenes that authenticated the kinds of statistics I'd been reading about television. I didn't like what I learned was true:

- By the time an average American child is eighteen, he or she will have seen 200,000 violent acts and 16,000 murders depicted on TV.[4]
- Parents spend 3.5 minutes each week in meaningful conversation with their children; the average child watches 1,680 minutes of television each week.
- The number of thirty-second TV commercials seen in a year by an average child: 20,000.[5]
- The number of TV commercials seen by the average person by age sixty-five: 2 million.[6]

Jewish cultural critic Max Antby writes, "Television does not exist to entertain us; it exists to sell to us." Antby quotes Georgetown and University of Maryland professor Colman McCarthy who said, "It is a commercial arrangement, with the TV set a salesman permanently assigned to one house, and often two or three salesmen working different rooms."[7]

The glowing television can be a distraction that we've stopped noticing, like the bark of a small dog that has shared our home for a decade. "Oh, that. That's just Scrappy," we say, waving at the noise. "I don't even notice it anymore—he's always barking like that. Don't mind him."

Studies have shown that kids younger than six usually can't distinguish between commercials and program content.[8] After I unplugged, I liked knowing that my children weren't drinking in and growing accustomed to messages that sounded to me to be the antithesis of what I wanted our lives to be about. I hoped that children who didn't see many commercials might grow up to be people who tread more lightly on the planet than they might otherwise have done, using less resources and given to fewer consumeristic whims.

I also hoped they would be happier.

In her brilliant movie *The Story of Stuff*, environmentalist Annie Leonard reports that each of us in the US is targeted with more than three thousand advertisements a day. Having the TV unplugged silenced at least most of these for my family and me. Leonard's research shows that Americans now see more advertisements in one year than people fifty years ago saw in a lifetime. She writes, "And if you think about it, what is the point of an ad except to make us unhappy with what we have. So, three thousand times a day, we're told that our hair is wrong, our skin is wrong, clothes are wrong, our furniture is wrong, our cars are wrong, we are wrong but that it can all be made right if we just go shopping."[9]

Leonard details how more commercials and more shopping actually makes Americans less happy. "Our national happiness peaked sometime in the 1950s, the same time as this consumption mania exploded," she writes. "We have more stuff but we have less time for the things that really make us happy: family, friends, leisure time. . . . And do you know what the two main activities are that we do with the scant leisure time we have? Watch TV and shop."[10]

I didn't pontificate about our choice and didn't want to be Self-Righteous, TV-Free Mom. (Remember the danger of those labels?) But I was glad the television was no longer casting its own particular spells on our family life. Without it, things changed for the better. David and I returned to activities that filled up our younger, pre-children lives. We lingered over cups of decaf coffee in the evenings, went on walks, and played Scrabble. I felt grateful that we'd unplugged.

When people learn that my kids have grown up without TV, they look at me strangely as though we use an outhouse instead of indoor plumbing or that I weave all my kids' clothes in homespun yarn. They talk about the benefits of educational programs such as *Sesame Street*. I agree, and I tell them I used to borrow videos and DVDs from the library so my kids could count with the Count and sing along with Elmo.

"You homeschool them, right?" they ask, eyeing me suspiciously.

This seems a logical question to ask, for many people. (Um, for both my own sanity and the health and well-being of my children, I have never seriously entertained the idea of doing so.) I think the assumption is that the reason I got rid of the TV was that I want to keep my children in a bubble, unsullied by outside influences. This isn't the case. (You should see our DVD collection.)

Every parent has a distinct set of resources, convictions, and preferences. We learn as we go regarding what activities, traditions, and practices help us connect with our children and help them thrive. We also learn, by trial and error, what defeats us in our attempts to raise healthy, happy children. Every family I know puzzles out those yesses and nos in their own way. Some *do* homeschool their children. Others opt out of standardized testing in schools. Still others avoid weekend sports commitments, and some families even make Sunday a true day of Sabbath. We are all different, and we make myriad personal decisions as we craft our family cultures.

In the interest of full disclosure, to say I've raised the kids in a TV-free home isn't exactly what it might sound like. It's true we don't have televisions in our bedrooms. It's (usually) true that during school weeks, the rule is "no screen." But on weekends, we watch movies together. I stream TV shows such as *30 Rock, The Office,* and *Arrested Development* and sometimes watch episodes with my older kids. I would even argue that *Arrested Development*, well-written and full of quirky characters thrown into ridiculous situations, imparts valuable lessons about integrity and the importance of family. All three programs provide keen insight into American popular culture, and they make me laugh until I snort.

Regarding the choice to minimize my family's exposure to commercials by ridding us of the TV, I echo the sentiments of Ellen Currey-Wilson, author of the hilarious memoir *The Big Turn-Off: Confessions of a TV-Addicted Mom Trying to Raise a TV-Free Kid,* who writes, "I don't want to make parents feel guilty for plugging their kids in. I know what it's like to need a break as much as the next stressed-out mom. Unfortunately, if the latest studies are at all predictive, a child hooked on television is more likely to have a life filled with tutors, medications, diets and counseling, and that hardly gives parents the guilt-free break they need and deserve. . . . But not everyone has to jump on the bandwagon. When parents simply remove the television sets from kids' bedrooms, positive changes occur."[11]

Things are different than when my kids were really little and I yanked out that cord. Back then, we didn't have TiVo, streaming, or other options for avoiding commercials. Watching TV required sitting through all of those ads; there was no getting around it.

Now there is.

Early on after my TV breakup, I worried that my kids would miss out. After all, I'd been raised on television and the movies that were shown on it. *The Brady Bunch, The Jetsons*, and *Family Ties*, among countless others. My brain is full of superfluous information, such as the names Bandit and Cledus, which, of course, don't come into use very often unless you are pretending to be a trucker on her CB radio when she is playing with walkie-talkies with her friend at a shopping mall at Christmastime. But, as usual, I needn't have worried. Despite not being able to sing the tune of the latest Oreo cookie commercial, my kids all have turned out just fine.

A few days ago I had lunch with a woman I've known since high school. Like me, she is in her early forties. You might say midforties, but let's not split (gray) hairs, okay? Like me, she is the mother of four children and, like me, she has watched her high parenting standards and ideals crumble and fall away as the years pass with each subsequent child. She remains mindful about nutrition, manners, and raising kids who respect themselves and others. But as we looked back on the way we parented our oldest children, we laughed at our formerly perfectionist selves. Many of the things that once seemed *critical* to us now seem, well, kind of ludicrous.

No refined sugar until she's five!
Nothing but collared shirts and khakis to school!
Only Mozart or other classical music on weekdays!

"You learn to pick your battles, right?" my friend asked me, smiling. I nodded. Then, in a flurry of motion as the people beside us stood to leave and a waiter poured water into our glasses, I missed part of something she said. She held her hand up, her palm facing me, her fingers spread wide.

"I have it down to just five key things now," is what I thought she said.

I almost dropped my fork: she'd crystallized everything that mattered about raising children into five essential things? Was that even possible?

"Five? What?" I sputtered.

She laughed when I told her how I'd misheard her. We began brainstorming the idea of what would be those five essentials of parenting and family life? It's a difficult exercise, to be sure. I mean, if someone wrote a book after truly discerning the five essentials of raising kids, he or she would sell more copies than a hot, new Amish novel.

"One would be love," I said. "I mean not only telling them I love them, but snuggling them. Even when they're older."

"Absolutely. I still hug and kiss my kids. They need it."

"Yep," I said.

"The second thing could be spiritual grounding," my friend suggested. "Praying with them, giving them opportunities to know God better."

"Agreed."

"Three could be books," I said. "Teaching them, as much as possible, to love to read. Not just because of what it does for them in school, but just because it will be something they'll always enjoy."

"That's right. And it's easier with some kids than others. Some are natural readers," my friend said. "Others, not so much. You have to encourage them. You have to let them catch you reading too. Work it, you know?"

"Amen!"

We never quite figured out what the last two items on the "five essentials" would be, but instead launched into a conversation on the proven benefits of reading.[12] Reading helps us learn to express ourselves, helps to develop imagination, and—yes—children who read more do better in school. They have longer attention spans, build bigger vocabularies, and understand cultural references in ways their nonreading peers do not. But when I try to make reading a part of my family culture, I know I'm giving my kids much more than an educational vitamin.

I'm giving them a friend.

Books are companions that usher us through difficult times or away from the inevitable periods when the world isn't going our way. Most of us, at one time or another, will be stuck standing in a long line. Trains will be late. Flights will be canceled. A friend will betray us. We'll sit for hours at the car dealer while someone investigates why that warning light is flashing. I mean, we could contemplate the cans of motor oil stacked nearby, play a mindless game on our mobile phones, or . . . read and be transported away from those brittle plastic chairs and the brash reality show on the TV above our heads to a small mill town in Georgia where a deaf man named John Singer listens to his young friend talk about her dream of buying a piano.[13] We could travel far from the strip mall to a coffee plantation in Kenya[14] or wander in a Savannah square, Spanish moss hanging eerily from the trees.[15]

Yes, I can live with my kids wearing T-shirts to school, having occasional sugar highs, and staying up too late on school nights from time to time, but reading has got to be a big part of all our lives—and having a family culture where TV isn't a barking dog we've all learned to ignore does help.

It only takes staying in a hotel for a few days to remind me why I'm glad not to have ready access to the TV in my home. A few weekends ago, I was in Annapolis, Maryland. Ian, my lacrosse-playing son, had a tournament there. In the evenings, while he and his teammates ate copious amounts of french fries (not dyed blue, I'm happy to report) and ran around the hotel, I stayed in my room. I attacked my e-mail inbox. I called friends who live in the area and caught up with them. I also did something I rarely do—and put my feet up on the bed and clicked on the TV.

As I mentioned, I'm a terrific channel surfer. I find it highly pleasurable to click through a hundred stations, getting a split-second sense of what's on the show. This time, however, I slowed down. It had been so long since I'd seen "real" TV. Was it really all that bad? Maybe I'm just an old Debbie Downer when indeed the quality of programming had improved. Maybe TV now was a bastion of excellence. I slowed down and took a look.

One station was playing *The Wizard of Oz*. Now who can complain about that? I savored the scene of Dorothy oiling the Tin Man's rusted joints and then started the progression through the channels.

Immediately I went from "Why, it's a man, a man made out of tin!" to a reality show on which a woman is tearfully telling the story of her husband's murder. By his brother. Who had shot him in the head. You see, the wife and her brother-in-law were having an affair, the details of which she very openly shared on this program.

Toto, we're not in Kansas anymore.

I clicked away from that one.

Next up was a program describing how to make sombreros. Helpful as that is, I didn't think I'd have occasion to need this information anytime soon, so I changed the channel.

Next I saw a commercial for a wrestling show.

Click.

A car race called *Super DIRTcar.*

Click.

A snippet of a sitcom on which a woman laughingly calls the man beside her a "meth-daddy" and talks about getting "butt naked" together.

Click.

Next was one of the *Back to the Future* movies. (Hi, Biff!)

Click.

Next was *The Story of Stuff*'s Annie Leonard's worst nightmare. It was a lengthy commercial that shows two women chatting and shopping at a huge discount store, their carts overflowing. One remarked admiringly about the massive amount of stuff her friend has in her cart and the other bragged that because of a special payment plan, she didn't even have to think about paying for any of it for *six months*! (*Wow! Six months! That's like half a lifetime!*)

I changed the channel.

I skimmed past a college football game, a boxing match, and then football again.

Next was a television drama on which a character was describing the domestic abuse she had suffered. She tearfully confessed that she was sure she deserved it.

The last show I saw before Dorothy and her friends lit up the screen again could be seen as a nightmarish sequel to the commercial of those two women and the overloaded shopping carts. Called *Hoarding: Buried Alive*, this reality show featured people who, on one level, were just obeying the call of their culture to buy, buy, buy. (Many hoarders also suffer from obsessive-compulsive or other mental disorders, so of course there's much more to it than a love of shopping.) They purchased mountains of "stuff" in a desperate attempt to make themselves happy and whole. There were stacks of clothes, still on their hangers. There were microwaves, toys, garbage, and canned foods stacked floor to ceiling in their homes. The occupants of the houses were ashamed and isolated. All the things they had bought had been rendered useless by damage and decay.

That the show was darkly called *Buried Alive* disheartened me.

I turned off the TV.

CHAPTER 7

Overheard at the Wedding Reception
Adventures in Eavesdropping

The boy is a miniature version of his father. Together, they walk into the restaurant, wearing matching tuxedos and shiny black shoes. Their dark hair is spiked and gelled in the same style. The father appears to be about thirty years old; the son looks about two and a half. They make a handsome pair.

At first glance, it appears they are holding hands, swinging their arms, but as they approach, I see that the man is pulling his son into the room. The boy jogs to keep up with his father's long strides.

The restaurant's huge windows overlook the golf course. I'm sitting alone, writing in my journal and enjoying a quiet lunch while my sons spend a few hours with friends, learning to play golf somewhere out of my sight on this huge course. It's been an idyllic summer afternoon, but now I notice a large patch of dark sky approaching. A storm is threatening.

"Look!" The boy points out the window. "Water pool." He speaks in a chirpy voice, high and sweet.

"It's not a 'water pool,'" the man says gruffly. "It's a lake. And just so you know—I don't care. If you could just behave yourself, we'd be back in there at the wedding."

"Big water pool!" the boy says happily, undeterred by his father's displeasure. His little hands press against the glass as though he's willing himself to pass through it and float above the lake. "Water pool!"

"I. Don't. Care," the man says, speaking each word as though it were a sentence of its own. "I don't care about water pools or lakes. Why were you so noisy? Why couldn't you just behave?"

The boy ignores his father's questions. "Daddy! What that?"

"What?"

"In the water pool, what that?" The boy is pointing and jumping up and down.

"It's a fountain," the man says. "And that's not a water pool. It's called a lake."

"Fountain, fountain, fountain," the boy says, throwing his arms into the air, imitating the water that is spraying up from the middle of the lake.

The man sighs and sits down at a nearby table.

When my husband, David, has been short-tempered with our children, he sometimes tells me the story of his outburst start to finish. As a preface, he explains to me that what he's about to disclose "is not what you'd call an award-winning dad moment." Often, if he has lost his temper, it's after one of our kids has repeatedly ignored his requests, or another was unkind to a sibling. Midway through the story we begin to laugh at the way kids can infuriate us and that we sometimes end up acting like children ourselves. Usually the story ends with the way he has apologized to the children for losing his temper and how he revoked—or at least modified—the cruel and usual punishments he initially meted out. (*No allowance for a year! No playdates until you're in middle school!*)

Laughing helps.

At those times, I am slow to judge David. After all, how many times have I lost perspective or my sense of humor with one of the children? Can I even count that high?

Likewise, despite this man's grumpiness at the wedding, I bet he's a good father. He's understandably frustrated, of course, and probably just spent an embarrassing quarter of an hour trying with all his might to quiet his child during a wedding ceremony.

But I can see that his child is bright-eyed and curious. The little boy is accustomed to having his questions answered and to being listened to by the adults in his life.

My bet is that this boy has calm and loving parents, *most of the time.*

The boy walks to his father, whose head is in his hands, tugs at his sleeve, and leads him back to the window.

"Daddy! What that?"

"Nothing. Just the fountain and the water pool," he says.

I can't help but smile. The boy has won; his father has unwittingly adopted the phrase "water pool."

"It's a bug," the boy says while scratching his fingernail against the glass, trying to touch something on the other side.

"It's not a bug," the man says. "It's a smudge."

"A fly!" The boy slaps the glass. "Go away, fly."

"It. Is. Not. A. Fly," the dad says, his staccato words indicating his rising frustration. "It's dirt. Just dirt on the window."

"Go away, fly," the boy shouts.

"You are *incorrect*. It is not a fly. It is dirt," the man says.

"I no *incorrect*," the boys says, a challenge in his voice. "It is a fly."

"You know what Daddy did?" The dad puts himself between the boy and the window and bends down. He now speaks in a serious tone. "Daddy hired a car. It's coming in one hour to take you and Grandma back to the hotel."

"Yaya!" The father's bad news doesn't have the desired effect. The boy is delighted.

"You can't be here with Daddy and Mommy anymore. You were too noisy. You have to go back to the hotel with Yaya."

"Play games with Yaya?"

"Yes," the man's voice softens. "You can play games."

"My Yaya!" the boy says, jumping up and down. "My Yaya."

"You'll have a good time with Yaya," the man says quietly. "Now, can we go back in? Can you behave yourself? Can you?"

"Bye-bye, fly," the boy says.

"It's not a fly. It's a smudge," the man says. He picks up the boy and whispers something to him. The boy nods and wraps his arms around his father, hugging his neck.

"Now we are going back in and you aren't going to make a sound. Do you understand? Not. A. Sound."

As they reach the doorway to the wedding service, the boy turns around in his father's arms.

"Bye-bye, fly!" the boy yells.

The dark patch of sky is overhead. Sheets of rain hit the windows and then disappear as quickly as they've come. The sky lightens and the golfers, undeterred by the brief summer storm, continue their games.

CHAPTER 8

On the Bwight Side . . .
Adventures in Mistaking Kids for Mini-Adults

When my son Ian was little, I sometimes worried that he was a sociopath. No—wait—let me rephrase that. That's too strong. I sometimes worried that he was an egotist. Or a narcissist. Or somehow lacked compassion. You see, from the time he could speak until he was three or four years old, when one of his siblings fell down, bruised a knee, or otherwise was physically or emotionally hurt, Ian would remark, unperturbed, "Well, *on the bright side,* that didn't happen to me."

To be completely accurate, due to a speech impediment that prevented him from pronouncing the hard *r* sound until he was about five, it was, "Well, on the *bwight* side . . ."

As I held the injured child, his or her tears soaking through my shirt, Ian regarded the situation, delivered his commentary, and slipped past us. I knew the child in my arms would recover; I was more concerned about Ian. *Will he ever learn to be empathetic? How in the world do you teach compassion? Will he ever exhibit concern for the needs of others? If the sight of his baby sister's skinned knee doesn't emotionally affect him at age three, will he ever care about the suffering of others?* I mean, he had seemed to adore his sister since the moment he first saw her after she was born. Why wasn't the sight of her tears devastating to him? Later I'd try to get through to him, in a calm yet firm manner. "You know, earlier, when Isabel fell down, it really hurt her."

"Yah. Hew knee bleeding. She was cwying and cwying and cwying," he'd observe. "But, *on the bwight side—*"

"Yes, I understand you're glad that *you* aren't hurt. But Isabel's feelings matter just as much as yours do. When Isabel gets a scrape, it stings. You can think about how you would feel if it were you."

"Yah. But it *wasn't* me," he'd clarify, obviously relieved that this was the case.

"But how would it feel if it had been you?" I'd press.

"Guess it would huwt," he would say with a shrug, and then he'd be on his way.

The next time someone fell off his bike or bemoaned the loss of her favorite stuffed animal, my cheerful little son would once again say, "Well, *on the bwight side . . .*" I'd shake my head and wonder what in the world I was going to do to disabuse him of the notion that his were the only feelings in the whole wide world that mattered.

But I need not have worried. A year or two later, I stopped hearing that refrain. When one of his siblings was hurt, he would rush to bring a little treat such as a favorite stuffed animal or a lollipop. "You want to hold Tigey?" he'd ask his sister, offering the comfort of his favorite toy. "Tigey can make you feel better."

Fast-forward ten years, and Ian is an emotionally intelligent and caring boy. He has a gift for working with children and becomes a one-man vaudeville show when he's with a young child who is fussing or sad. He throws himself down in pratfalls and makes silly faces that, inevitably, make little children forget whatever was troubling them. Kids delight in being around him, and it's mutual. He uses this affinity for kids to help others; it's a gift. A few days ago, for instance, I received an e-mail from the director of children's ministries at my church. She wanted to let me know how kind Ian had been to a child during Sunday school.

"Ian was sort of a big brother to one of the little boys with special needs," she wrote. "You would have been proud to see him in action. Just wanted to share that with you, and please pass along my appreciation to him!"

That's who Mr. "On the Bwight Side" has grown to be.

I wish I'd known in those early years of parenting not to worry so much. I wish I hadn't seen everything my little ones did as somehow predictive of what they would do as adults.

If she's telling a lie now, does it mean she'll perjure herself someday?

If he's fidgety now, will he never be able to sit through a history lecture in college?

If he's this obsessed about the ice cream truck, will he end up toothless and morbidly obese, the floor of his house littered with stained Popsicle sticks?

In a *Newsweek* article titled "In Defense of Children Behaving Badly," child development expert Po Bronson writes, "It's widely accepted in our society today that young kids' behavior is a window into their future. . . . However, it turns out not to be true. One simply must be very careful prematurely judging early childhood behavior."[1]

In the story, Bronson cites a study that compared the short- and long-term effects of two different disciplinary styles. Some parents demand obedience from their young children, while others use reasoning tactics in their parenting. Small children who are forced simply to comply with their parents' orders exhibit better behavior than kids with less authoritarian parents, Bronson writes. However, when the same children are older, the children who were reasoned with reap benefits from their parents' approach. "Long term, encouraging kids to reason scaffolds complex thought, language development, and independent thinking

. . . children of parents who appeal to reason turn out better," Bronson concludes.

So when your child's teacher expresses concern that your kindergartner is restless at reading time and doesn't immediately plop to the floor and sit cross-legged in a box drawn with masking tape on the floor, don't despair. Explain to your son that being a good listener is important. Perhaps point out that others will be better able to focus on the story if everyone is sitting quietly and still. But don't decide the boy will never finish high school. It's way too early to predict such things.

Bronson notes that young children aren't gifted at reasoning (*I want it now! That's mine!*). It would follow, then, that Mr. "On the Bwight Side" wouldn't be able to put himself in someone else's shoes either, no matter how often I asked him to do so.

As a young mom, I also sometimes mistakenly thought that my kids' interests as little children pointed directly at what they'd be drawn to as adults. When he was four, a very stern Theo approached me after we'd gone to the library.

"You need to teach me to read," he said, gesturing at a pile of picture books. "It's not fair that *you* can read and *I* can't."

As previously established, I'm a bit of a book nerd, so his demand came as a pleasant surprise. I went online to find out what I could about teaching kids to read and asked homeschooling friends for their recommendations. In the end, I purchased a book called *Teach Your Child to Read in 100 Easy Lessons.*[2] It *was* easy! It worked! Theo and I had fun doing the lessons together and although the authors caution parents not to complete more than one lesson of about ten minutes a day with their children, sometimes we sat on the couch going through the book for an hour. Theo insisted that we "Keep going!" By the time we reached the last page of the book a few months later, Theo was reading at second-grade level.

Mission accomplished!

Two years later, when Ian turned four, I sat him down and opened up that trusty manual.

"Good news!" I said. "Today I'm going to start teaching you to read."

"No, thank you," he said, sliding off the couch.

"Hold on. Come back up here," I said, patting the spot beside me. "You see, when you know how to read, you can pick up *any* book and read it."

"I like it when you read to me," he said, sliding down again.

"Oh, yes. Me too! And you and I will still do that, just like I still read to Theo," I said. "But look how much he loves to read books all on his own too!"

"That's okay, but I don't want to do it," he said.

I finally managed to convince him to read through a lesson with me. Just one! (A bribe of some horse stickers may have been involved.) He sat still, relatively speaking, as I enthusiastically went through the lesson. At the end of it, he asked me if we were done and then slipped away as quickly as possible.

The next day when I asked him if he wanted to do his reading lesson, he shook his head.

"No, thank you. I'm going to go play," he said.

And that was that.

Now, you might assume—as I did on that day—that while Theo became a wonderful reader, Ian was destined to lag behind his brother. You might wonder, as I did, whether I should have forced Ian to do the next ninety-nine lessons. Perhaps—here I nod to proponents of extreme parenting—you think I should have called him names or withheld his dinner until he agreed to do the reading lessons.

Well. I didn't.

And guess what?

It worked out just fine.

Although it *is* true that Theo was reading well when he started kindergarten and it wasn't until he was in first or second grade that Ian became a full-fledged reader, in time it all evened out. And actually, when given an afternoon with nothing to do, it's Theo who goes for a run, downloads songs for his iPod, or otherwise occupies himself. Ian is the one who is ten times more likely to flop onto his bed and read a book. (His current passion is reading military history, mostly on World War II. The kid knows more about blitz-krieg tactics and the invasion of Normandy than anyone I know.)

I somehow had come to believe that my sons' early childhood behavior was, as Bronson describes it, a "window to their adult selves."[3] I thought of them as pocket versions of their adult selves. Of course, they are so much the people they were from birth: Theo's focused gaze, Ian's merry spirit, Isabel's strength, and Mia's sweet temperament. But every year they come to understand themselves and their place in the world in new and ever more profound ways.

When we think children are mini-adults, we make all sorts of assumptions about childhood. Fortunately, I've been disabused of that notion again and again by people who insist that kids are, well, kids. One such truth-teller was Ian's third-grade teacher. I'd heard rumors about her before learning that he was assigned to her class. She was too laid-back, some parents complained. Instead of learning the fifty states and capitals the traditional way (Maine? *Augusta*! South Dakota? *Pierre*!), she had her students perform a play. A musical, no less!

I don't remember much about the play except that the words *great* and *state* were rhymed together quite frequently and that one little girl turned green during the performance and I thought she was going to vomit. As soon as I noticed her pallor, I began nudging and "psst"ing at her mother, who didn't have a clear view of the girl. Other parents scowled at me and thought I was being a rude audience member, but finally I got the mother's attention, did some rudimentary sign language, and she slipped up the side of the room, pulled her daughter off the risers, and ushered her out of the room.

Just in time, if memory serves.

Anyway, Ian's teacher told us on curriculum night that if there ever were a day when our children had homework but we were in the mood to take them on a bike ride or play a game with them instead, we should just write a note explaining why the homework wasn't done.

"They grow up so fast," she said. "Enjoy your time with them."

Now before you blame teachers like this one for the downfall of the American economy, you should know that she is a gifted teacher, and I saw Ian grow academically by leaps and bounds that year.

But she was a little . . . nontraditional.

When I mentioned at our parent/teacher conference that Ian's handwriting seemed sloppy, she looked at me incredulously.

"He's in *third grade*," she said, laughing. "Take it easy, Mom!"

It was, in fact, a relief to have this teacher. I didn't have to pretend to care about things that I knew were not important. I didn't have to hustle to make sure this homework sheet or that project was done perfectly. Ian loved going to school, came home bursting with ideas, and when I had the compulsion and energy to take Ian and his siblings to the park after school, I could do so with a clear conscience.

Now if you prefer more of a Tiger Mother parenting model, you might be extending your claws when you hear about his teacher. This was certainly the case for some of my friends. They whispered on the playground about their concerns. What if third grade was meant to be their child's make-or-break year and it was compromised because of this teacher?

Taking that worry to the next level, one might ask what if, because of an only patchy knowledge of state capitals, one of our kids would someday miss a few points on the SAT and then fail to be admitted to an Ivy League school? What if then he would fail to meet the friend who would have otherwise been the ideal business partner? Meanwhile, thanks to the "Great State" musical, our children will be relegated to community college instead of attending Harvard.

What if?
What if?
What if?

A few nights ago at dinner, Ian told me a story about this teacher. He had learned in school that day that she was one of the first people who taught a young man named Mawi Asgedom[4] after his family arrived in the US from Ethiopia. They were refugees, unfamiliar with the language, culture, or educational system. I bet his teacher's warm, creative classroom was a very good thing for Mawi and his mother! Mawi, Ian said, learned English quickly from this teacher and flourished in her class. Later he graduated from Harvard University and even gave the speech for the graduating class. So, whether or not his third-grade teacher made him write neatly or memorize state capitals, I'm thinking Mawi ended up doing pretty well.

I asked him, "Hey, Ian—what's the capital of West Virginia?"

"Charleston," he answered, rapid-fire.

"Delaware?"

"Dover. Why do you ask?"

"Oh, I was just remembering that musical you did in third grade."

"*Fifty Great States*," he said. "Man that was a fun year."

"You learned a lot," I said.

"Yeah," he said. "I loved it. And remember how poor Emma almost threw up during the musical? She turned green."

My friend Mark, when he speaks about his childhood and adolescence, often ends the story by saying, "It takes a long time to grow into who you are." He knows that. From a chubby kid who sometimes felt invisible, he became a powerful actor and teacher. But he was raised in a time—for better or worse—when children were not viewed as mini-adults but simply as children. Just . . . children. Mark's words are a reminder to me. This child's gifts or that one's weaknesses are not reliable predictors of how they will fare in life. It takes time to grow into who we are.

Our culture, though, points at the naked emperor—also known as the odd way we are deforming childhood—and says, "Ooh. Nice outfit!" But as parents, we can resist that message, point at that silly figure, and say, "Nope. He's got a whole lot of nothing on." Kids *do* keep growing and changing. Kids *don't* need to be as serious about their studies in third grade as does a thirty-year-old doctoral candidate. They don't even have to aspire to attend an Ivy League school.

Now that Theo, my oldest, is in high school and edging up to graduation and the next phase of his life, we talk about college. By fifteen, he was already tired of adults asking him where he was planning to apply. He gathered a few unlikely school names that he has been tempted to use as answers when overeager adults ask him that question.

"Where do I want to go to school? I was thinking about the Colorado School of Mines. Or the London School of Hygiene and Tropical Medicine. Or maybe Panhandle State."

When I first started thinking about Theo and college, I fantasized about what it would be like *for me* if he went to a prestigious university. "Oh, Theo's away at school this fall," I'd say, letting out an opulent sigh. "Yale. I'm so happy for him. New Haven is just *lovely* in the fall." (Can't you just see me in my "Go Bulldogs!" sweatshirt?)

"Oh, yes, it is a good school!" I'd say. "He's a bright boy. You do recall that I taught him to read when he was just four years old." At that point I'd toss my head, perhaps casually tucking a strand of hair behind my ear.

Luckily for all of us, I knew steering my son toward a school simply because of how it would make *me* feel to say he went there was a really, really bad idea. And if I have attempted to raise kids who are not obsessed with brand names, who are authentic, and who will seek to serve others with their lives, that would have been just plain wrong. I decided I wanted to do better for him than pushing him toward the college with the biggest name and highest "Aren't I a successful mom?" quotient.

While browsing at a local bookstore, I happened upon a terrific book called *Colleges That Change Lives: 40 Schools That Will Change the Way You Think about College.*[5] *Aha!* I thought. *This is more like it.* In the book, author Loren Pope busts every myth I had always believed to be true about helping my kids choose a college. *No*, he says, your child doesn't need to go to an Ivy League school to be successful in life. In fact, none of the Ivies is included among the forty colleges Pope picked as life-changers. He promises that these lesser-known and often smaller schools "will do as much, and usually far more, than any status school to give you the rich, full life." The best schools, he explains, focus on the aptitude of their *graduates*, not of the students at the time of their college admission. Such schools understand that kids aren't "done" at eighteen, but will learn, grow, and mature throughout the college years.[6]

After reading Pope's book, I went from wondering whether I was failing Theo as a mom by not pressing him to go to a high prestige school to feeling a sort of wonderful relief that there are *many* good schools in the US and he will certainly be admitted to one of them whether or not it's in the Ivy League. The book gives me the freedom, like that wonderful third-grade teacher so many years ago, to let my teenage child be a teenage child. Theo can enjoy high school. He can keep studying hard most of the time (after all, it was Theo himself who said, "What you do *most of the time* is what matters") while continuing to give himself room to socialize, play, and just relax. He can go to football games with his friends. Play pick-up soccer games at empty fields around town. Listen to his iPod.

I will help him prepare for the college entrance exam. I will keep insisting that he uses "whom" when he should. ("Object pronoun!") And when it happens, as it did just last night, when he asks my advice about whether he should take a high school course he's interested in even if it's not A level and won't carry as much weight on his grade point average, I will say, "Yes! Take it!" (The class, by the way, is "The History of Rock & Roll in America." According to the course catalog, it "provides students with the opportunity to explore the history, creation, and development of Rock & Roll. As music has played an integral role in societies across the globe, Rock & Roll has helped to define American culture over the past century. This course will allow students to discover the history of Rock as they analyze social trends, movements, and events that led to the development of American popular music in the 21st century." Um, I'd want to take that class if I were him.) The point is, I'm certain that whatever the outcome of his applications in a few years, everything is going to be all right.

None of my kids is done maturing yet. The human brain just keeps developing. One set of studies says we aren't truly mature adults until we reach the age of twenty-five.[7] *Twenty-five!* Still, sometimes we expect preschoolers to be empathetic, to be selfless, and even to respond graciously when another child grabs their new sand shovel at the park. Instead of shouting "Mine!" we'd rather they respond like well-bred adults. ("I say, friend. I was just constructing a castle and using that tool. Would you mind returning it to me?")

No—they wail, grab the shovel back, and possibly fling a little sand in the direction of the perpetrator.

It's actually a good thing that children start out in life behaving as though their needs are not only the *most impor-tant* ones in the whole world, but the *only ones*. If babies and toddlers weren't always bellowing about being hungry, tired, or injured, how would the adults in their lives know to meet these needs? Can you imagine a three-year-old who cut his hand on a piece of broken glass rationally looking at the situation, realizing that it wasn't a great time to bother his mom while she made dinner, and just let it bleed? Or an infant lying in her crib in need of a clean diaper and dealing with hunger pains but thinking, *Oh, I woke them up an hour ago. They must be exhausted! This can wait.*

Or a toddler saying, "Oh, hey. I didn't want to trouble you earlier, but I think I'm allergic to bee stings. My arm has swollen up quite a bit. If you have time later, would you call the pediatrician for me?"

As much as we fantasize about such things on endless, sleep-interrupted nights, it would not be a good thing. No— young kids perceive their hunger, injury, and well-being as the most important things in the world. And that's how it should be. They are vulnerable. They don't know how to use a cell phone and take-out menu when they're hungry. They need our help and protection and care.

By all of this, I'm not saying we shouldn't engage in the long and, yes, tedious process of teaching them manners, modeling generosity and restraint, and disciplining them for misbehavior. (Throwing sand in the sandbox really is a no-no.) I just mean that we don't need to think that because they aren't naturally selfless, they are destined to a solitary, vain life. Or that if they'd rather run and play than do reading lessons when they're four, they'll never learn to read. They aren't fully mature, remember, until they are twenty-five years old!

I know that, despite the fact that a child's nature will determine much about him or her, parenting does indeed matter. Kids who are connected with their parents *do* get better grades. They *do* engage in less risky behavior. They *do* bring more good to the world. There's a lot we can't control, but we can teach our children by word and example how to treat others. We can help them learn to be resilient. We can model to them that they are valuable and that every person deserves their respect. We can praise them for their efforts to do well. We can teach them to seek redemption—in their social and spiritual lives. With our help and in spite of our mistakes, as we parent them with love our children will keep growing and changing, becoming more independent, more empathetic, more the people God has created them to be.

But we don't really *need* to teach them to read when they're four years old.

(Unless, of course, they insist on it.)

Take This Quiz with Your Kids

. . . and then look at a developmental chart[8] to be reminded that it takes time for brains to mature and for kids to learn everything from block-stacking to empathy.

Behavior	Child (birth - 3 years)	Child (4 - 24 years)[9]	Adult (25+)
1. Sometimes resists sharing			
2. Likes to please friends			
3. Likes to sing and dance			
4. Smiles spontaneously, especially at people			
5. Can stack two blocks			
6. Runs stiffly, sometimes with eyes on ground			
7. Seems selfish or contrary at times			
8. Confuses notions of "want" and "need"			
9. Can jump in place, but sometimes loses balance			
10. Feels entitled to the last piece of garlic bread			

(Um, I don't know about you, but I checked every box in the 25+ column.)

CHAPTER 9

Eating Dinner
Adventures in Breaking Bread

I have a friend, Peter, who lived for several years in the Middle East, in Baghdad and Dubai. He is currently attending seminary in the United States, preparing to be ordained as a Roman Catholic priest. Last summer, as the two of us sat at his kitchen table and ate crusty bread topped with double-cream brie and drank good pinot noir, he told me that eating together is considered an act of worship by his Muslim friends.

"In the Middle East," my friend said, "people who are merely acquaintances do not 'grab a meal' with each other. Eating together is too intimate an act to be shared with strangers."

It had been a weekend of breaking bread together for Peter and me. Earlier that day, after spending a few languorous hours browsing used bookstores, we had stopped for afternoon tea. The previous evening, Peter had taken my recently minted teenage son Ian and me out for dinner in his Massachusetts village. The restaurant Peter chose was walking distance from his house. It was a small, upscale bistro with striking artwork on the walls and fresh sea scallops, lobster, and many other delicacies listed on a hand-drawn menu.

"Ian, my friend," Peter said, after we were seated. "I would like you to order whatever you'd like tonight. *My treat.*"

My treat. Is this not one of the kindest phrases in the English language?

Hearing this, Ian leaned back in his chair, ran the palms of his hands over the menu on the table in front of him, and sighed contentedly.

"Ah, well. Let's see," my son said.

Peter has the courtesy and charm of Stephen Fry's character Jeeves in the British television series *Jeeves and Wooster*, based on P. G. Wodehouse's short stories. Like Fry's Jeeves, Peter is tall and dark-haired. He tips his chin down, peers over the reading glasses that sit near the end of his nose, and smiles. Often his is a quizzical smile befitting a person so in love with observing—and redeeming—the human condition.

As Peter and I chatted at his kitchen table in Massachusetts, Ian sat in the next room, watching one of the Catholic DVDs that Peter had recommended to him.

My friend has a not-so-secret plan to convert my family to Roman Catholicism. He shows my children icons, sends us biographies of the saints, and has demonstrated how he prays with a rosary.

"You would be such good Catholics," he says wistfully. "I pray for you every day."

But I'm content with my own faith tradition and—in my mind, at least—it is one not so very different from my friend's. We have the same doctrine about Christ. Our liturgical services, to the uninitiated, can look almost identical. While Roman Catholic priests perform Mass from the *Sacramentary*, Episcopalians celebrate Holy Communion using *The Book of Common Prayer*. Both Protestants and Catholics use the terms *Eucharist* and *Holy Communion* interchangeably. The word *Eucharist*, by the way, comes from a Greek word meaning "thanksgiving, gratitude."

As a Christian, I'm more than a little embarrassed to note how vehemently those in my faith draw the lines between our denominations. Sure, Catholics have the pope, venerate Mary the Mother of Jesus more intentionally, and interact somewhat more frequently with the saints than those in the Protestant church do—let's be honest here. Both groups claim a belief in the divinity of Christ and in his death and resurrection.

Those are pretty substantial beliefs to share, if you ask me.

As a person with many friends who are, at best, bemused by my Christian faith and speak of it courteously, as though I had a strange, inexplicable obsession with ceramic seahorse figurines, I like to look at what we Catholics and Protestants have in common. For instance, Catholics and Episcopalians recite the Nicene and Apostles' Creeds. Both churches administer baptism and celebrate the Holy Communion. *I know, I know.* I'll get people on one side saying I'm not really a Christian for having even made those comments and others whining that I've brought up that embarrassing Christ thing, that *peculiar seahorse collection*, again. Oh well. I'm no theologian. (Obviously.) But when Peter tells me about his fervent prayers that I "convert," I refrain from saying what I'm really thinking.

"Convert to what? *Rastafarianism?*"

Alas, back to the Eucharist.

On Sundays in our church, the service for Holy Eucharist begins with readings from the Bible, followed by a homily given by the priest, the exchange of greetings among those in the pews at the peace, and then Holy Communion. Like many meals shared by families and friends—including those I've shared with Peter in Massachusetts and elsewhere—the ritual begins with an expression of gratitude to God. The priest says, "Let us give thanks unto our Lord God" and the people respond, "It is meet and right so to do."

The priest then reads the account of the Last Supper and reminds us that in receiving Holy Communion, we remember Jesus' death and passion and we are able to partake, mystically, in his body and blood. Christians understand this differently; some of us believe that the bread and wine used in Holy Communion *literally* become Christ's body; some of us believe those two elements serve as symbols. Regardless of one's theological particulars, we agree that receiving the bread and wine is a sacred act.

So what's the connection between Ian's artfully arranged plate of sea scallops in that Massachusetts bistro and the wafers and wine that are given to whomever approaches the rail at my Episcopal church (or at my friend Peter's Roman Catholic seminary)? I like to think that there is a strong connection between the two, even though one is generally deemed *social* and the other *spiritual*. When we kneel at the altar rail or sit together at a table for dinner, we are present with each other. We are all on the same level—age, race, and social class are rendered unimportant. It strengthens us, as family.

My friend Dr. Grace Freedman, a public policy expert and mother of three, thinks family meals are so important that she has started a nonprofit organization called eatdinner.org to promote it. Among eatdinner.org's many findings are that families who often eat together are more likely to have healthier diets, consume more fruits and vegetables, and feel more satisfied and connected in their relationships. She's also gathered data to support the claim that children and teens who frequently eat dinner with their families are more likely to do well in school, be at a healthy weight, and report having a good relationship with their parents. Such kids are also less likely to use drugs and alcohol and less likely to have disordered eating or depressive thoughts.

Some of the details she's found include that:

- Teens who had dinner with their families on a regular basis were more likely to get As and Bs in school (64 percent reported these grades among those having dinner five or more nights a week). Teens who have dinner with their families fewer than three nights a week are twice as likely to report getting Cs, Ds, or lower grades in school.[1]

- Frequent family meals are associated with a lower incidence of depressive symptoms and suicidal thoughts, as well as better grades in eleven- to eighteen-year-olds.[2]

- Adolescent girls who have regular, frequent family meals are less likely to have eating disorders and extreme attitudes or behavior about weight control.[3]

But how many of us do eat together? Eatdinner.org reports that, according to Pew Research, only about half of families make dinner a daily ritual and another third eat together a few times a week. About one in five families eat together only occasionally or never. Although there has been an increase in family meals in recent years, there has also been an increase of children "doing other activities" while eating, such as watching TV.[4]

"American families are confronted with many urgent social, economic, and health challenges today, including obesity, teenage alcohol and drug use, tight budgets and time constraints made worse by the recession, and feelings of disconnectedness among family and friends. Family dinner can be a solution to many of these problems. The simple act of having regular family meals has been shown time and again to have positive effects on children, teens, and their parents on a broad range of issues related to social, emotional and physical development," Grace Freedman writes.[5]

I met Grace and her husband, Michael, about eighteen years ago, appropriately enough at a corporate dinner. Michael and I worked for the same company in Manhattan. Over the years, we have broken bread together several times, including at their wedding and at the Seder dinners they held in their Brooklyn home, not far from where David and I lived before we had children and moved to Chicagoland. The first time I ever celebrated a Passover Seder was with Grace and Michael. On the walk to their house that evening, David and I stopped in at our local wine shop. There were two kosher varieties of red wine tucked into a dusty corner.

"Do you recommend either of these?" I asked the shopkeeper. He shrugged and gave me the same wincing smile that Mike exhibited when I presented them with the kosher wine later.

"Yeah, it doesn't really have to be kosher," Mike tactfully noted. The Freedmans are Reformed Jews.

(Hey, I grew up in Wheaton, Illinois, where there is

a church on every corner. What do *I* know about Seder customs?)

The Seder feast, as *you* likely know, is a Jewish ritual that marks the beginning of Passover. It's observed within a faith community or generations of a family. When I attended my first Seder dinner at Mike and Grace's house in Brooklyn, Michael's father led the conversation. He described the emancipation of the Israelites from slavery in ancient Egypt and told stories I had heard all my life, ever since Sunday school days. I remembered singing, as a young child:

> *When Israel was in Egypt's land,*
> *Let My people go!*
> *Oppressed so hard they could not stand,*
> *Let My people go!*

Celebrating Seder brought those songs and stories of my childhood alive. I loved the slow, relaxed rhythm of the evening and the way my questions as a Christian Seder newbie were thoroughly answered. Michael's father explained the symbolism of the foods on the table. The salted water for the people's sweat and tears. The bitter herbs for the bitterness of slavery. And the unleavened bread, the matzo, reminding us that the Israelites fled Egypt in such a hurry that they didn't have time to let their bread rise. Matzo symbolizes the redemption and freedom and grace God granted the people in ancient times and offers us today.

Whether I look at family dinners as a sort of sacrament,

or simply as a tool in raising healthy children, I know I have to make them a priority. By "priority," I don't mean to imply that we all eat together every night of the week. We don't. But, *most nights*, we manage to make it happen. After school, the kids eat big bowls of Cheerios or Life cereal before they run off to sports or music lessons, but when we all return home, sweaty, tired, and sometimes out of sorts after a long day, we wash our hands, sit down together, and say a word of thanks.

On mornings when the calendar warns that the day ahead is the kind that will spin out of control until evening, I retreat to my basement freezer. Inside are half a dozen loaves of french bread and several big containers filled with chili, minestrone or split pea soup, and shepherd's pie. It's my little vault, a stash of meals that I cook every few weeks on Sunday afternoons to reheat for dinner on hectic days. On such days, I set the bread and soup out to defrost on the stovetop in the quiet house as we all scatter for the day's activities to be heated up when we are all home again.

It *matters* that we eat together; doing so keeps us connected. Eating dinner together helps us get a glimpse into the details of each other's lives. It helps the high school sophomore remember what it was like to be in fourth grade, like his sister is now. She talks about her teacher reading *Super Fudge* to the class. Her older brothers and sister speak over each other, laughing, telling their favorite parts of the story. The younger kids listen, rapt, as the intricacies of middle school romances are explained. My husband and

I talk about our work and, month after month, our kids follow the ups and downs of our careers, know the cast of characters of our professional lives, and are happy with us when we have good news to share.

Every night that we eat together, we play a game called "Best and Worst." I've heard it called "Highs and Lows," "Roses and Thorns," and "Highlights" by other families. We go around the table and say, in a sentence or a paragraph or a short treatise, what was the best and worst moment of that day.

Sometimes my kids' bests are good grades on a test. A funny game one of them played at recess. Beating his or her best time at a track meet. Playing well in a soccer game. That it's Friday. Worsts include homework. The argument that just ensued with his brother before dinner. That we are having soup again. My daughter Mia usually gives her best, thinks a moment, and then announces, "I don't have a worst." (I love to hear that.) If we weren't sitting together at the dinner table, rolling pasta around a fork or lifting a soup spoon to our lips sharing stories, ours would be a family less connected than we are. Eating together is a gift we give ourselves and is one for which I am very grateful.

It *is* indeed a kind of Eucharist.

Now having said that, I should note that dinner at our house is not as formal as kneeling at the altar in church or sitting in a fancy restaurant with my bachelor friend. There is no wait staff, except my husband and me. There is no incense and no chanting. In fact, often before we have a chance to say a prayer of thanks around the table, one or more of the children have already sat down and begged, "Can we start?" Or, without asking, some have pilfered cucumber slices or cherry tomatoes from the salad bowl or have inhaled a piece of bread. When they were younger, I likely would have ground the whole dinner hour to a halt if such infractions were committed, lectured them about courtesy to the chef (me), gratitude to God, and all manner of other matters that would have sounded like that Charlie Brown *mwah-wah-wah-wah* talk to them.

But now I am aware that when my high school son sits down to dinner, he has been awake for about thirteen hours. He ate breakfast at 6:15 a.m., had lunch at 11:30 a.m., and now sits down for dinner at 6:30 p.m. Yes, perhaps he had a granola bar or a bowl of cereal after school about 2:30 p.m. before soccer practice, but when I grab a Sharpie and he and I visit the wall by the back door every few months, I am amazed when I draw a new line another half inch up the wall. The marks on the wall and the quickly outgrown sneakers suggest to me that his body is changing. And fast.

So if it's dinnertime and his father hasn't arrived home from work yet or his sister is insisting that she is really, truly *almost* done with her homework and he's hanging around the table, his stomach growling so loudly you'd think you could hear the plates of the earth shifting, waiting for the rest of the family and this selfsame kid inhales a few pieces of garlic bread before the rest of the family sits down and we thank God for the meal, I'm content to look the other way.

"Can I . . . ?" he begins. I nod.

He knows I'll nod.

So you could say that's not very Eucharistic.

But then when we are all at the table, we might sing together:

God is grace and God is good,
We do thank him for our food.

Or we say a prayer from the prayer book.

Or, most of time, one of us goes off road and thanks God for the day, for the pasta, for the dog, that Grandma is better from her cold . . . It's during long and rambly prayers that I sneak a peek at the kids to make sure they aren't swiping another piece of garlic bread while everybody else's eyes are closed.

Of course, sometimes they are.

Countless travesties have occurred at our dinner table over the years that would make the pope blush. (Okay, not really, but I just wanted to mention him in the interest of Protestant–Roman Catholic relations.) There was the time when Ian dramatically vomited eggplant Parmesan onto his plate after being forced to take "just one bite," thus tainting the dish in the minds of the other children forever.

At our dinner table, there have also been countless glasses of spilled milk. It's funny what makes us see red as moms. For me, spilled milk or the occasional glass that drops to the floor on its way from the dishwasher to the cupboard doesn't upset me. "If it wasn't a frequent occurrence, there wouldn't be a saying about it," I say, tossing the perpetrator a dish towel or broom.

But when I find a sandwich crust primly neglected in a lunchbox, I want to scream. "Oh, really? We don't eat *crusts* now? We're too good to eat the crusts of perfectly nice bread? We just throw away food, do we? We think nothing of just tossing out bread crusts *in this world of hunger and suffering? Really?*"

(I'm a lot of fun sometimes.)

My point is, when I say that family dinners are a priority and when I talk about the connection that is strengthened when we all sit down together, I am telling the truth. But I don't want to paint an idyllic picture of neatly groomed children unfolding their napkins onto their laps (though they will usually do that when I remind them) and making conversation about the wonders of the night sky (although I do think we've talked about that once or twice) or holding forth in an intelligent manner about politics.

Dinner, for us, is much, much more casual than that.

During dinner, we go on silly riffs such as the one recently when the kids labored to create a tagline for my youngest, Mia.

"You're the youngest kid in the family, like Michelle Tanner on *Full House*," Theo said. "You need a tagline. A little something you say in response to everything. Something we'll all get sick of but think is funny anyway. Your own special phrase."

At the time, my daughters were hooked on the program and had dipped into their saved allowances and birthday money to buy a boxed set of *Full House* DVDs.

"I don't want a tagline," Mia said.

"It would be cute," Ian said.

"Really cute," Theo agreed.

The boys were teasing her, baiting her, and drawing her out. (As a girl who grew up with two older brothers, I know this dance well. I also know it only does her good and that this attention secretly pleases her.)

"I don't want a tagline," Mia repeated.

"Like 'How rude!'" Isabel said, quoting *Full House*.

"Yeah, I get it."

"'Your pants are on fire,'" Ian suggested.

"How about, 'Hey you. Get offa my cloud'?" Theo said.

"I don't want a tagline," Mia said.

"'That's what *she* said,'" Theo added.

"I don't want a tagline," Mia said. She was starting to get frustrated. "I mean it."

"Okay, no tagline for Mia. Case closed," I announced.

The children not only tease but also interrupt each other. They have been known to kick each other's chairs, tattle on each other, and jump up from the table to do all manner of impressions. It looks very little like Norman Rockwell's iconic painting of a family eating a Thanksgiving meal. And, honestly, I wouldn't change a thing. (Well, I would prefer not to have that eggplant Parmesan image locked in my memory. But other than that . . .)

As the kids grow older, of course, things have become more settled and polite, especially on those evenings when I make the effort to set our dining room table. Candles, a tablecloth, and the dimmed lights signal to the family that we have time to settle in. There's no rush to choose just one "best and worst" from everything that transpired that day. We breathe a little deeper when the textbooks and backpacks are out of sight. When we eat in the dining room, everyone seems to bring their *A* game. Because it's so relaxing, I aim for us to eat in the dining room at least once a week. Almost every single night, however, regardless of where we sit for dinner, when it comes around to my husband to say what was the best and worst part of his day, at "best," he grins and says, "Dinner. Definitely dinner."

Even when some milk—or eggplant Parmesan—has been spilt.

Author and food blogger Rachel Stone points out that "in the Bible, food is always a sign and sacrament of God's love and provision for his people." Jesus, she reminds us, "calls himself 'the bread of life.' And, Jesus did a lot of eating *with people! . . .* Eating together, in every culture, is a signal of belonging and acceptance."[6]

Stone writes, "When we eat with others, we sit on the same level with them, acknowledging our common crea- tureliness as we stop and do the necessary, joyful business of eating. When we eat the same food, the same food goes into each of our bodies, building up our cells, becoming, quite literally, a part of each of us. We may or may not share much conversation, but we are nonetheless bound to each other in breaking bread together. And Christ is with us."[7]

When my husband and I were newly married, we lived in Dallas, where we were in graduate school. We attended a small Episcopal church that announced from a prominent sign in the entryway "Our Church Has AIDS." It was a surprising and even jarring message to read on first entering a church, especially in the late 1980s. The sign made very clear to those who entered that this was God's house, a place that went by a different set of rules and guiding principles than the world outside. *All* were welcome here. What a bold and beautiful way to destigmatize a disease about which people felt such fear—to claim a church identity in that way.

It seemed to me that this kind of otherworldly love was just what Christianity was supposed to be like. When it was time for the Eucharist, I felt honored to walk the center aisle to the altar rail and receive the bread and the wine with people whose IV poles, thin bodies, and often marred faces revealed the fact that they were ill with what was the most socially taboo disease of the time. While, on the outside, people with AIDS may have been avoided or ostracized, this was God's house, a place ruled by a law of love. There we were, all approaching the altar to eat and drink God's love and gift of forgiveness for us.

That felt like real grace to me.

CHAPTER 10

Parenting after Orange Alert
Adventures in Living Bravely in a Fearful Time

Usually there were one or two, but on that Tuesday afternoon there were lots of fathers on the elementary school playground when school let out. The adults stood around, dazed and bleary-eyed under the vaulted, azure sky. The school's flagpole held the flag at half-staff. The dads on the playground had been sent home from work; some were in their good suits, their ties loosened. Some work in Chicago and were sent home so that skyscrapers would be empty should another attack occur. Other companies let their employees go because of the gravity of the day. One woman, waiting for her child to be dismissed from school, looked up at the perfect blue sky and announced, to no one in particular, "It's so surreal, walking over here after what's just happened."

It was, of course September 11, 2001.

My heart, like yours, was broken that day, shocked by the vigorous display of hatred. It *did* seem surreal to have images of smoke and death imprinted on my mind while all around me all I could see were quiet streets and neat lawns bordered by impatiens. Regular, ordinary life.

"Why did they cancel Scouts?" Theo, then a kindergartner, asked. "Was it the same reason Daddy got to come home from work early?"

"People thought it was a good day for families to be together," I said.

He looked up at the blue sky, nodded, and smiled.

"Yes," he agreed.

At home that afternoon, my boys found a slug in the dirt as my husband sat in the wooden swing in our backyard.

"Look at this, Mom," Theo called, holding the slimy thing between two fingers.

"It looks like a snail," Ian said. "It has antennae."

I slipped inside to check e-mail. I didn't want to tie up friends' phone lines in New York but wanted to touch base with the people I knew there. I wanted to make sure they were all right. My friend Grace Freedman's husband,

Michael, worked near the World Trade Center. She sent a short note. "It's devastating, but we're OK," she wrote.

My husband's brother, Brian, called in tears from London, where he was on vacation with his wife, Sara.

"It's an effort just getting my shoes on, you know?" my mom said over the phone, her voice heavy with grief.

I heard from my friend Laurie, who works for American Airlines at O'Hare airport. She said the airport was eerie, the usually busy runways transformed into a giant parking lot for planes, the terminals quiet. She was dreading seeing the crew lists from the crashed planes. They were the names of people she knew well.

"There was a bad fire in New York," my neighbor told her five-year-old son. The boy's uncle worked in Manhattan and, after hours of watching television and trying to phone him, my neighbor finally got through to her brother. I decided to follow her lead and told the boys that there had been a fire. There was just no way to explain it to them.

"There was a fire. People are sad. The firefighters were brave," I told them. Both boys' faces lit up. They had been to the fire station only months before on a tour. Firefighters were *already* their heroes. No duh they were brave—of course they were! (At the time we had two goldfishes. Ian had named his "Cowboy"; Theo's was "Firefighter.")

During dinner, the boys chattered about the slug and baby Isabel tossed tomatoes off the tray of her highchair. I stared out the window. The absence of planes in the sky felt oppressive. I missed the familiar, muted thunder of their engines and was suddenly aware of how often, since becoming a mother, I watched airplanes pass by on the highway over our heads.

"Look! It's an airplane!" the boys were always shouting, as though each time was the first time they had seen one overhead.

All day, I slipped out of the room and I watched the towers come down, over and over, on my computer. Theo asked me why I put my hand over the screen when he came into my office.

"Hey, are you thirsty? Remember the lemonade we made this morning?" I said, changing the subject.

In the evening, my mother-in-law called to say that the brother of one of my high school friends was on the plane that crashed in Pennsylvania. That scene of a phone ringing, of terrible news being delivered, repeated all across the country. Precious family members lost in a blitz of unspeakable hatred and violence.

They said it over and over again. "Nothing will ever be the same . . ."

Now, of course, all four of my children know about 9/11. Their schools recognize the anniversary of the attacks with special assemblies and lessons. Although I've tried, I've never quite been able to articulate to the children the cruel way the rules changed when instead of using a bomb to kill innocent people, the terrorists used innocent people to be part of a bomb that would result in such ghastly destruction and fear.

The effects of that day endure and, since then, we continue to digest discouraging news, often related to those acts of hatred. Wars. Global warming. Al-Qaeda. Hurricanes. Tsunamis. Mudslides in California. Terrorist attacks in India. Airlines filing for bankruptcy. A quadruple-dip recession. European debt crises. The way we have to take off our shoes and strip down at airport security and stand in the body scanner, our hands held up above our heads almost in the shape of a heart as though we were a tweenager at a Justin Bieber concert. The dangers of high fructose corn syrup and trans fats. Everywhere you turn there is another caution, another disease or social ill becoming prevalent, or another headline that feels like a punch to the gut.

I grant you that al-Qaeda can't be blamed for mudslides, tsunamis, and trans fat in our food, but still . . . it's a dispiriting time, and I find myself with that common malady of compassion fatigue. I want to escape. I am drawn toward light entertainment and silly movies. Maybe I should give *There's Something about Mary* another try! I want to avoid thinking about famines, conflicts, and tragedies of every sort.

But I also want to stay awake and to hope.

I can't help it—hope is built into my DNA and a key part of my Christian faith. Remember the passage that was read at my wedding? *Love hopes all things.* And love, we read over and over in the Bible, casts out fear. The angel said to Mary, "Do not be afraid" (Luke 1:30). To the shepherds:

"Do not be afraid" (Luke 2:10). Do a search on that phrase in the Bible and you'll find it numerous times. When he appears to humans, our God of love often prefaces his messages with, "Do not be afraid."

As a mother, I want to raise brave kids who hear that message and know it to their toes. Everything is going to be all right. Love *wins*, as they say.

I want them to be people who know that there is a bigger picture, a spiritual promise of hope and redemption, even when life circumstances feel frightening.

I don't want them to lose sight of it or fail to see God's gifts of love around them because they are afraid of what, ultimately, cannot harm them.

Further, I have some good news for you: we are no longer living under Orange Alert. (Did you know that?) In 2011, our government scrapped the color-coded threat level system that since 2002 had warned Americans of the risk of terrorist attacks. The system was reminiscent of those signs out West that portray Smokey (the) Bear and announce the day's probability of forest fires. These are updated daily in the hope that, for instance, should a person see that there's an *extreme risk* of forest fires on a particular day, he won't throw a lit cigarette out of his moving car into the brush at the side of the road. "Only *you* can prevent forest fires!" Smokey says. Knowing how to respond to the Homeland Security warnings, however, was much trickier than making sure campfires are extinguished properly.

The threat of Orange Alert, or a high risk of terrorist

attacks, loomed over our heads for years. (The only thing that could have been worse was a Red Alert, but those didn't pop up too often.) In April 2011, however, the colors were washed away in favor of a new system. Personally, I wish that just for a brief, shining moment, Homeland Security could have made a quick announcement that we were at Green Alert, or a low risk of attacks, before wiping the slate clean, but alas, it was not meant to be.

Now, should there be an imminent terrorist threat, we will learn about it via the National Terrorism Advisory System, or NTAS. The new terrorism prevention message that replaces the color warnings is reminiscent of the "Loose Lips Sink Ships" campaigns during World War II. "If You See Something, Say Something,"[1] it urges. The slogan reminds us that the enemy may be anywhere.

For most of us, as parents going about our days at work and with our children, it's hard to imagine that we're part of an antiterrorism effort and that members of al-Qaeda could be lurking around the corner. Sure, if you see a neighbor stockpiling explosives in his garage or if you observe him timing traffic lights, you might get suspicious and certainly should let authorities know. But for most of us, this won't be the case. As far as I know, the only stocking up my neighbors do involves multipacks of paper towels and breakfast cereal from Costco. But still, we're cautioned: "If you see something, say something."

I wonder how living under so much fear and vague warnings since the terrorist attacks in 2001 has affected the way I raise my children. If the suicides in Jonestown frightened me so much as a child, how much more are children growing up now affected by what they learn about those attacks? The people who died on September 11, 2001, were not misguided zealots who had chosen to leave everything they knew to follow their leader to a South American country. They were all just ordinary people going about their ordinary lives.

It's not always easy to be brave, despite my best efforts.

I find myself part of a typical scene after dinner. It is a moment when in the mix of ordinary life, I fight to remain present, to force worry and fearful thoughts from my mind. Ian begins a long opening argument of why he should have more dessert. He points at his empty dinner plate. He suggests options. *Just a bit of sherbet. One square of dark chocolate. That last cookie.* He walks around the kitchen, looks in the pantry, examines the shelves in the freezer, and ignores my repeated offers of a banana or yogurt.

The other children chat about school. Isabel reportedly tried the hot lunch that day and to her surprise, she loved it. I ask her what she ate and she speaks each item in a velvety voice as if she is a waitress listing the specials at a five-star restaurant. *A blue Popsicle. A big salad with croutons. A blueberry muffin. A bag of carrots.*

"And *chocolate* milk," she finishes with a sigh.

Mia is relegated to her chair until she finishes her milk. She stands up and then, when directed by her siblings or me, sits back down again. "Drink. Your. Milk," I say for the sixth time. (Hey, quit your complaining, kid—it isn't powdered.)

Isabel asks to be excused and disappears down into the basement to a bin of cleats, baseball socks, and pants. Tomorrow night she has her first game. She emerges from the basement with a few pairs of softball pants. I ask her if they are the right size. "They're fine," she says. "I wore them last year, all the time." Since last season, she'd gained something like fifteen pounds and grown about four or five inches.

"Why don't you try them on," I say.

She shrugs and takes them into the bathroom.

Ian, meanwhile, continues his negotiations. He notes that there is only one cookie left in the package. Maybe, he wonders aloud, it would be a good idea to split it with his brother. *Finish it up, you know, and recycle the package.*

Mia continues to refuse to drink her milk. She picks up her glass and raises it, but before taking a sip, she again speaks of about the newborn goats she saw that morning at a local zoo.

"They were born last Wednesday. In the evening," she says.

"Drink your milk," I say.

Isabel returns wearing a pair of softball pants. They are uncomfortably tight and barely reach her knees.

"I'll get you new ones tomorrow," I promise.

Ian walks up close to me and brings his index finger to one of his eyebrows. He notes that his brows are growing thicker.

"See, here?" he says.

"People get hairier as they grow older," I say.

"You're getting hairier because you are turning into a monkey," Mia explains, the glass of milk again raised in her hand.

We all break into laughter, but Mia nods to herself matter-of-factly, glad to have clarified the situation. I look at each of my children, my heart aching with love. I wish I could grab hold of the evening and freeze it in time. The repeated requests for more dessert. The outgrown pants. The milk (finally) dribbling down my daughter's chin. The dirty dishes still on the table. The upside-down bottle of Ranch dressing. The dog wandering in and out of the room, checking under the table for fallen bits of food.

It's beautiful to me, and I'm aware of how precious it all is.

But I can't keep this moment.

Usually when time is frozen, it's because something terrible has happened. Otherwise, life moves on in its ordinary, unobtrusive way. Gray hairs appear at the temples where they haven't been before. Kids grow taller between the times we stand them against the wall and mark their heights. The bulbs we planted last fall send shoots up overnight and, when we aren't looking, they bloom. But when something awful happens, time stands still.

Hurricane Katrina. Shootings on college campuses. An earthquake in Haiti. Car wrecks. 9/11. In the days that follow such tragedies, we look at pictures of the victims. Even strangers' faces affect us. We know each one is someone's child, precious and loved like our own. Children whose parents limited the number of cookies they could have for dessert, made them finish their milk, kept them in clothes that fit, and experienced countless moments of regular, ordinary life with each one of them.

We realize how priceless each life is.

We wish there was anything we could do to turn back time and make things turn out differently.

My sons erupt into laughter, yanking me from my thoughts.

They repeat their little sister's pronouncement over and over: "That's because you're turning into a *monkey*!"

Mia smiles, raises her glass, and finishes drinking her milk.

Despite the anxiety of the times, the way we mess things up, and the challenge of raising hopeful, optimistic kids in a post-9/11 world, we roll up our sleeves, plunge in, and say yes to family because, as clinical psychologist and author (and yes, television personality) Dr. Phil McGraw says, "family matters."

"Family matters because it is the single most outcome-determinative factor shaping one's outlook and achievement. Your family powerfully determined what you've become and how you think about yourself, and so it will be for your own children. That's why among all words in the English language, none means more to human beings than 'family.'"[2]

Amen!

A (Sort of) Serenity Prayer for Mothers of Young Children in an Anxious Time

God, grant me serenity—just a little serenity.
(Once in a while and for a few minutes, at least.)
Midweek would be ideal because, as you know, dear God,
by Wednesday night, my sense of humor is
running on fumes.

Give me courage, God, at the grocery store,
When the baby is crying and I have to
pick up a few things for dinner.
Guide my child's outreached hand
toward the natural granola bars,
Not the ones that contain trans fat,
high fructose corn syrup, and food dye.
(Lord, I confess, I do not always have the
wisdom to know the difference.)

Keep me from making irrational conclusions
about my children's behavior, Lord.
Let me remember that just because he grabbed
a handful of chocolate-covered raisins
from the bulk foods bin,
my three year-old is not destined for life as a shoplifter.
Help me recognize that just because she
drew on the dining room wall, Lord,

My kindergartner will not spray paint graffiti on the sides
of buildings when she is a teen.

Help me not to see danger around every corner
Or to be afraid of my world, dear God.
It is, after all, your creation.

Help me not to fear the shadows,
But help me to send my kids into the world as the
Beautiful, light-bringers that you made them to be.

Most of all, as I mother these children
who are your gifts to me,
Grant me your peace.

Amen.

CHAPTER 11

Overheard on the Bus
Adventures in Chaperoning Field Trips

I'm prone to eavesdropping. So, given the chance, is every mother I know. (*Shh . . . don't tell!*). We mothers become expert at blending into the background and listening in when we're driving carpool or sitting on a school bus full of kids as a field trip chaperone. Being surrounded by our kids and their classmates and friends, staying silent as they tease each other, gripe about coaches and teachers, and whisper about whom they do or do not have a crush on that day provides a rare and clear window into their worlds. (It's an education.)

You've heard about middle school, right? About the regimented social hierarchy? The frightening bullies? The "mean girls"? The teachers who cuss and criticize? In my experience, middle school can include some of those things, but it seems to me that more significant than locker or teacher or boy/girl troubles is the fact that kids this age have one foot firmly planted in childhood while the other strains toward becoming an adolescent.

What an anxiety-laden place to inhabit!

A recent ride I took on a school bus full of middle schoolers reminded me of this, renewed my appreciation for my own children, and resulted in my being exceptionally kind to my tween kids on their arrival home from school that day. I'd gotten a glimpse into their world, and I felt only compassion for them.

I'll share my *Harriet the Spy* notes with you here.

I didn't know the two middle school girls sitting in the seat in front of me on the bus. They looked much like all the other girls to me. Hair pulled back in ponytails. T-shirts and jeans. Fleece jackets. Braces on their teeth. They were definitely caught in that uncomfortable place between childhood and adolescence. They were alternately graceful and then awkward. Mature and silly. Confident and viciously insecure. My own child sat a few seats toward the back of the bus. To spare him embarrassment, I refrained from turning around and looking at him. If I did, I'd have to crane my neck around the side of the seat like the mom across the aisle was doing to see her son.

"Hi, sweetie!" she called.

He ignored her.

"Sweetie, hi!" she called, louder this time.

"*Mom*," he said, as though he was responding to his mother having danced an Irish jig or shown his baby pictures to the kids on the bus. She shrugged and sat back down in her seat. I was not a first-time middle school mom. I dutifully remained facing forward, opened a book, and bowed down to the pages, pretending to read.

"That substitute had coffee stains on her teeth," one of the girls in front of me said.

"And coffee breath," her friend agreed. "That was gross."

Coffee breath. I slipped my hand into my purse and felt around at the bottom of the bag for a mint. I silently tore the wrapper and carefully transferred it to my mouth.

"And then did you see? She took a bite out of that chocolate that wasn't even for her. My friend brought it back from vacation. For the *real* teacher."

"She was mean," the girl said.

"I like that other one."

"Mrs. Hettinger? She does the lesson and talks about books she likes. Sometimes she plays games with us."

"Yeah. She's okay."

They were quiet for a moment.

I wished I knew this substitute teacher so I could tell her the fond way these girls speak about her. My reverie was broken when one said, "That Ryan farts a lot."

The other agreed. "He's kind of fat too."

"He's huge!"

"And he sweats."

"*Shh* . . ." The girls sat up tall on their seat and peered over the seat past me.

When they turned around again, I glanced to see if Ryan was on the bus. I didn't remember seeing any enormous, sweaty, gassy boys in the vicinity. I hoped he hadn't heard these girls.

"Did you do that jump rope thing in gym? We were jumping this cool way—you know, one rope, two people?"

"I'm bad at that."

"I'm not."

"I am. It's hard."

"I'm kind of harsh on myself. And other people too."

"I'm mean sometimes, but not as bad as my sister."

"My sister makes me sound like an ogre. I'm not an ogre. Usually."

"I don't like it when people meet my sister before they meet me. I like it when they meet me first. Not like 'Oh, yeah, I know your sister.'"

"I thought you were really scary when I first moved here. I was going through this shy phase. And you were always with that Bethany."

"I hate her. I don't know why she hangs around with me."

A teacher made an announcement from the front of the bus. Whoever was playing music from his cell phone needed to turn it down. All the kids around me looked around and laughed.

"Remember what we talked about at school," the teacher warned.

The girls sat down and continued their conversation.

"I thought you were friends."

"What?"

"You and Bethany. You seem like you're good friends."

"Yeah. We are. I guess I don't really hate her."

"She's nice."

"Yeah. She's really nice."

"What did you get on that Egypt test?"

"It stinks. She gave me an 80."

The girls again sat in silence for a few minutes.

"Hm. Who else do I hate?" one of them murmured.

"I don't hate people, but some people really annoy me."

"Who else don't I like?"

"I like your phone."

"Put your number in so we can text sometime."

"Okay."

Listening in, especially on tweens and young teens, fills me with compassion—and even pity!—for the time in life my kids are wading through. On days when I help at the school, I'm more likely to hug them a little longer when we're home again. To sit and focus on them. Ask them about their days.

"Do you know a kid named Ryan?" I asked my son after school.

"No. Who's Ryan?" he answered.

"Never mind."

CHAPTER 12

Baleen Whales, Taco Night, and the Cheese Stick Bubbler
Adventures in Creating Family Lore

The way you sing "Oh, What a Beautiful Mornin'" when you wake up your kids. How your kids like ketchup on macaroni and cheese. Letting the cats roam the kitchen counter. Going berry-picking every summer. Game night. The brand of toothpaste you use. Breakfast dinners. Celebrating Chinese New Year. The three different brands of peanut butter you keep in the pantry. Placemats. Public television. Country music. Thai food. Knock-knock jokes.

Whether or not we're aware of it, as we raise our children we're creating our own unique family cultures. Each is its own entity, crafted from traditions we bring from our families of origin, souvenirs from our travels, and the people we meet. Ideas gleaned from books.

One element of my family culture is the practice of holding family meetings at least once a month. Every few weeks, on Sundays at six in the evening, I call David and the kids to the living room for our family meeting. On their way, the children make a detour into the kitchen to pick up their drinks. Somewhere along the line, 7-Up with maraschino cherries, served in parfait glasses, became the signature drink for our kids during family meetings. David and I often pour a glass of wine, and I set cheese and crackers or other simple foods on the coffee table so that no one suddenly announces that he or she is "starving" during the meeting.

It is, most nights, a structured, courteous occasion when we look ahead to the week, discuss upcoming vacations or special events, alert the rest of the family about arriving guests or changes to our routine, and just talk together. If your kids are very young and the thought of sitting everyone down for a well-ordered family meeting seems impossible, please remember that my kids are all in the double digits now and things weren't always so composed.

Not by a long shot.

When Isabel was a baby and the boys were four and two years old, I read in a parenting book about the importance of holding regular family meetings. Family meetings bring families closer, help children learn to express their opinions, and serve as a vital component of happy, healthy family life. *Start when they're young*, the author directed, *or your kids might not be willing to participate when they are older.* This, of course, struck terror in my heart. If I *ever* wanted my family to reap the benefits of family meetings, I knew I needed to commence them *right away.* (Even if two of the children were still in diapers.)

You won't be surprised to hear that our first family meetings bordered on the absurd. There was Isabel in her high chair crushing graham crackers onto her tray as the boys and I sat around the dinner table. (These were in the days when David traveled a lot for work. Despite his absence, I feared that if I didn't start immediately, I'd miss my window and we'd never get into a rhythm of successful family meetings. So, without my husband, the tradition began.)

"Tonight is our very first family meeting," I announced. The boys sat in their booster chairs, regarding me with interest. "We're going to talk about family rules and expectations, and then we'll just brainstorm about what kind of family we would like to be. Okay?"

"Okay," they agreed.

Isabel pointed at the cracker box. I gave her a few crackers, hoping they would occupy her.

"I'd like us to be a peaceful family," I said. "Peaceful in our home and peaceful with our friends."

"Okay," they said.

(Well, *that* was easy!)

"Do you have any ideas about rules for the family?"

"Don't push," Theo suggested.

"Great! Don't push," I said. "That's a good rule."

I had brought a yellow legal pad to the table, and wrote "Don't Push" on the first line. Both boys took note, pleased to see that their ideas were being written down. In the next minutes, they were full of ideas for me to transcribe.

"No hitting!" Ian said.

"No whining," Theo added.

"No playing in the stweet!" Ian shouted.

"No breaking things."

"No pushing!"

"I already said that," Theo said.

"No pushing *down the steps*," Ian said.

"That's still pushing."

(Can you see how later they would be able to find a way to fight about body hair?)

"Okay. Thanks, you two," I said. I had sort of hoped that the "rules and expectations" would be more nuanced. Maybe be more "Golden Rule" and less particular regulations. Alas.

"Do any of you have any other concerns you would like to share?" I asked.

The boys smiled politely at me.

"Like, for instance, if there are foods you like and we aren't having them very often for dinner, you could request them when we have family meetings like this. Or if you feel like some of the rules that Mommy and Daddy make aren't fair, you could tell us about that. Or if there is something you want to learn more about, you could tell us at family meeting and Mommy could find some books or activities to do about that subject."

"I like tacos," Ian said.

"Excellent!"

"I like tacos too," Theo said.

Things were going *so well*.

"So you would like us to have tacos more often at dinner?" I asked.

They nodded.

"Done!" I announced and scribbled "more tacos for dinner" on my legal pad. "Anything else?"

Baby Isabel held her hand over the side of her tray and let a cracker drop to the floor.

"I think bats are interesting," Theo said. "You know, because they are mammals but they can also fly!"

"Great!" I said, writing "study bats" on the pad. "We can learn more about bats. I think they're interesting too. Anyone else?"

"Cacka," Isabel said, letting another cracker drop to the floor.

"I like the caw wash," Ian said. (Remember he wasn't very adept at "r" sounds back then.)

"Me too, honey. Like when we pretend we've been swallowed by a whale when we're going through?"

"A *baleen* whale," Theo said. He was very serious about marine biology in those days. I, of course, was sure he would someday be an oceanographer when he was older. Because, you know, he liked whales so much as a preschooler. (Sigh.)

"Isabel scweams in the caw wash," Ian said. "It makes hew so fwightened. But *on the bwight side . . .*"

"Cacka," she agreed, either commenting on having dropped another graham cracker or trying to repeat the words "car wash."

After convening two or three such family meetings, at which tacos, sea creatures, and crackers were again repeated points of discussion, I decided that maybe the kids were still a bit young for family meetings. We did, for the record, make "taco night" a nearly weekly tradition that continues to this day. And I was able to find a class through the park district where the whole family made a bat house, learned about bats, and read books about them. The bat house still is nailed to a tree in our backyard. The squirrels like to stand on top of it.

So, there's that.

A few years later, when all of the kids could speak well and had stronger opinions about how they wanted the family to be run, our meetings were slightly more productive. We discussed table manners. ("Don't steal garlic bread when we're praying before dinner.") The kids shared their hopes. ("I want more playdates and we should have candy more.") Unfortunately, the meetings became contentious.

"At this family meeting, I would like to say that Isabel took my LEGOs," one of the boys would say.

"I did not!"

"And she used them in the fort she was building."

"I did not!"

"And when I told her to give them back, she hid them behind the red couch."

"I did not!"

I learned of broken plates, purloined cookies, and other crimes some member of the family had been trying to hide. When our family meetings seemed destined always to crumble into tattletale sessions or unpleasant arguments about stolen toys or other personal fouls, I decided we should take a short hiatus from convening them.

We picked them back up when all of the children were in school. Looking back, this would have been a perfectly reasonable time to have our first family meeting, but I was simply trying to follow the parenting author's guidelines. (Warning to readers: use common sense when you consider duplicating something you read about in a parenting book. Seriously.)

In our new series of family meetings, with all the kids in elementary school, we discussed and agreed upon family rules. We talked about favorite vacations, friends we'd like to invite over for dinner, and many other matters. We continue to use our meetings for such issues and also share our schedules and get the good—and the bad—stuff out on the table every week.

When I was in college, I was (in)famous for getting my friends to sit around and play "Truth or Truth." Like "Truth or Dare," it's an easy party game; unlike the original, in "Truth or Truth," there is no danger of being asked to sing "I'm a Little Teapot" or to eat a cookie with ketchup squirted on it. "Truth or Truth" is about connection. It's about getting to the heart of issues as critical as discovering what your friend would do if she only had twenty-four hours to live or the best restaurant meal she ever ate.

These days, our family meetings sometimes include a sort of "Truth or Truth" game. I often distribute questions and we all jot down answers to what is our best hope for the coming week or when in the week that has passed we felt most glad to be ourselves or what mistake we've made that we hope never to make again.

Recently I gave everyone a handout that read: "One thing people in my family don't understand about me is _____."

We then took turns, "Truth or Truth" style, sharing our responses.

"Just because I love reading about military history doesn't mean I'm obsessed with war."

"My feelings are hurt easily these days."

"I'm going through a lot right now and it's not always what it seems."

"Even though I'm a grown-up, I have feelings too."

"I love owls. I love them so much."

"Sometimes I'm quiet, but I'm still happy."

Like riding on the bus to a field trip or driving the carpool, hearing my husband and kids read their answers to these kinds of questions gives me insight and compassion for the members of my family. I'm grateful to know them all better.

Sometimes, when the new and old business has been addressed at family meeting, the conversation takes a more casual turn. One of the kids will start a conversation by asking, "Remember that time . . . ?" and then I know we are in for another hour of chitchat. It's then that we tell family stories, our own particular folklore. Every culture has its folklore. Telling, capturing, and sharing the stories that make a family distinct—and embarrass, amuse, and instruct us—is one of the joys of being a family. (It also passes the time when the power goes out or when we are on long car trips.)

"Remember that time . . ."

Sharing family stories brings healing and nurtures connectedness among family members. Whether the story is grim or comical, family lore is important. We repeat the same stories time after time.

The kids tease me about the day, in a blizzard, that I insisted we drive out to western Illinois and cut down our Christmas tree. David tried to change my mind, citing safety concerns and pointing to the cars that had spun off the road on our own block, but I was determined. The closed roads and poor visibility delayed us such that by the time we got to the farm, it was closed. So were all the cut-your-own-tree farms in the area. We returned home, the wheels spinning on the icy roads, and bought a cut tree a few blocks from our house.

Or there was the time Isabel found a dead fish floating in the lake by a cabin we'd rented. She fell in love with it and looked for its bloated corpse every time she swam or we went out in a boat. "Where's Bartholomew?" she'd call, worried for its safety when she didn't see it right away.

Or how I used to pull yellow marshmallow Peeps from the kids' ears when they were little; they were sure it was sheer magic.

Or the time I nicked Ian's ear when I was cutting his hair on our back porch as Theo, panic-stricken, sat nearby awaiting his turn for a haircut. "There was blood on the scissors, Mom! Talk about child abuse!"

Or that Mia used to rename herself "Sneakers" whenever she had a new pair she loved. She was forever convinced that she could run much faster in brand-new shoes; they had miraculous properties, she believed. She would challenge her older siblings to a race, and good kids that they are, they barely jogged to ensure that she would finish first.

We often remember the day I brought our dog Shiloh from the animal shelter after meeting a dozen or so much cuter, much healthier puppies. I had to call David from the car to tell him that our new dog wasn't one of the ones we'd seen on the shelter's website, but a very mangy, sick, pathetic little thing that somehow had stolen my heart.

"You're kidding, right?" David had asked.

"I'm not. Oh, and he just threw up in the crate."

"But he was the only one who didn't pee on you!" the girls say, delighted with the detail.

Or the time Ian bit Isabel's hand when she stole a pen from him and he received his first and last spanking.

"I remember that," Isabel laughs. "You left teeth marks."

"Didn't it bleed?" I ask.

"I don't think so," Ian says. "But then Dad came into my room and spanked me. I couldn't believe it."

"You deserved it," Isabel says. "And that wasn't even your pen."

"Poor Ian," Mia says. "Did it hurt?"

Or when a very young Isabel was convinced that Theo had somehow found a way to spit inside the string cheese wrappers.

"Theo bubbled my cheese stick," she shouted, after pulling apart the wrapper. "This cheese is *wet*!"

"How could I spit on your cheese stick when you just opened it?" Theo asked.

"I don't know, but it feels wet. Mom, tell Theo to *stop bubbling the cheese sticks*."

I was so amused by this unlikely dispute and so taken with the way she used the word *bubble* that I went online and made Theo a golf shirt with a tiny cheese stick logo and the caption "Cheese Stick Bubbler" on the front. The first time he wore it, Isabel stood in front of him, pointed at the picture of the string cheese, and then sounded out the words.

"Cheese stick bubbler!" she read slowly. "I knew it!"

I always wonder what my children will remember of their childhoods. The dead fish in the lake? That cold day driving in the falling dark to Christmas tree lot after Christmas tree lot only to find them closed? A spanking?

Memory experts report that children whose parents reminisce with them not only retain memories of their childhood but also have "better coping skills and higher self-esteem than those whose mothers don't." Psychologist Robyn Fivush at Emory University says, "We create a sense of who we are through these memories."[1] The game of "Remember That Time" then, is more than just a fun way to end a family meeting; it is one way we come to understand—and like—ourselves.

There was a first-grade teacher at my kids' school who died one summer just days before the school year started. Ian had been assigned to her class, knew her name, but sadly never had the chance to meet her. A new teacher was quickly hired to take her place. When the school year began, the other teachers were visibly shaken.

Years later, Ian would still say, "My teacher died when I was in first grade." He hadn't met her, but I believe that seeing the other teachers at the school grieving her death powerfully affected him. It revealed to him that teachers were real people with real feelings. And that they could die. Remember when seeing your teacher anywhere but in the classroom was a jarring experience? Many young children think the teacher exists only in one place and that is within the four walls of their classrooms.

When we'd received our class assignments the year

before, I'd mentioned to a friend that Ian had been matched with this particular teacher. It was before anyone knew she only had months to live.

"Oh, she's wonderful," my friend said. "You'll love her. She is so honest and matter-of-fact. One year an irate mother came in to complain after her son said that his teacher had told the class that nutrition and dental health weren't important and it was okay for kids just to eat candy for their meals."

"Nice," I said. "Like a teacher would say that!"

"Right. So the parent was really upset and came in and confronted her, but the teacher was unruffled. She just said to the angry mom, 'Look, let's make a deal. If you don't believe everything your first grader says about *me and my classroom*, I won't believe everything he says about *you and your household*.'" (Those words echo in my mind when one of my kids has told me an unlikely story about something that's happened at school.)

Words are mighty, and stories influence us, as that first grader surely knew. He probably thought he had hit on a genius idea: if he can create a world in which his *teacher* says eating candy for meals is a reasonable and healthy choice, then his mom will *have to* follow! He invented this wonderful world in which teachers preach *just* what six- and seven-year-olds most hope for . . . and that is that the base of the nutritional pyramid is constructed with *candy*! All of this, of course, was done only with words! That little boy had, maybe for the first time in his life, gotten a sense of the magical power of story. (And, no, I don't think that child grew up to be a liar or a thief. A novelist? An actor? A teacher? Maybe. I bet his teeth are just fine too.)

In Salman Rushdie's allegorical children's novel *Haroun and the Sea of Stories*, written when a death sentence had been issued on the life of the author by Iran's (Grand) Ayatollah Khomeini in 1988, story is revealed as the foundation for imagination, childhood, and joy. Without stories, characters in the novel become depressed, materialistic, and immoral. Even the relationship between the characters and the real world is deformed without stories.

"Africa, have you seen it? No? Then is it truly there? And submarines? Huh? Also hailstones, baseballs, pagodas? Goldmines? Kangaroos, Mount Fuji, the North Pole? And the past, did it happen? And the future, will it come? Believe in your own eyes and you'll get into a lot of trouble, hot water, a mess," Rushdie writes.[2] When those who hate storytellers are defeated, *peace* breaks out in the land. There is happiness and reunion. And Haroun's mother again begins to sing.

When my family and I tell stories—whether they are funny or painful or a mix of the two—we are shaping what we know about ourselves. We are becoming, with every repeated anecdote and snippet of family lore, more keenly aware of who we are and where we've been.

I love it when a sentence begins with the words, "Remember that time . . ."

CHAPTER 13

The Case of the Missing Clementines
Adventures in Faith and Compassion

The clementines were missing.

From November through March, I buy a crate of clementines along with our other groceries every week. *Darling clementines.* The kids take them in lunches and grab them for snacks. The little oranges are so healthy, user-friendly, and waste-free that I wish they would stay in season all year long. With the coming of spring, however, the price of these darlings skyrockets and inevitably when I throw caution—and my budget—to the wind to eek out just one more week of clementines, I find soft, moldy oranges hidden in the bottom of the box. But, in their prime, they are a simple pleasure and the empty wooden boxes serve us well all year long, as shelf organizers and craft boxes all around the house.

My love for the tiny oranges has sometimes even made me wish for another daughter, just so I could name her "Clementine." *Clementine*. (Wouldn't that be cute?) So far when I've had these momentary fantasies, something snaps me out of it. I hear a door slam or I get a text from one of my kids requesting that I find a missing library book or my foot falls on the sharp edge of a LEGO. I then come back to my senses. I remember that four children are enough for me and that having a child just so you can name her "Clementine" is a truly ludicrous idea.

Anyway, one winter a few years ago, I began noticing that our clementines were disappearing faster than usual. I'd set the box on the kitchen counter on a Monday and by Wednesday it was empty. I don't pretend to be good at math, but I knew that even if all four of my kids were eating two a day, the crate wouldn't empty that quickly.

One day, as she was doing her homework at the kitchen counter, I asked my daughter Isabel, who was in second grade at the time, whether she knew anything about the missing fruit.

"Isabel, do you know what happened to all the clementines? I just bought a box on—"

"Look," she interrupted, leveling her gaze at me and pointing her pencil at me as if it were a poison dart. "I just need them. And we are not going to talk about it." She gave me a final, fiery scowl, and then, satisfied that I wasn't going to protest, she calmly bent down over her homework again.

Now here's the thing. When I learned that I was pregnant with a girl, I began to pray that she would be strong. Too often in the world, girls are the victims of abuse and prejudice. Too often their gifts and very dignity are sabotaged. They receive the message that what *they look like* is the most important thing about them. They mask their intelligence. They doubt themselves. I do; so many of us do.

I didn't want to raise a daughter only to find that she was subverting her God-given talents to please or placate others. I hoped she would be good at math, would be strong and athletic, and would know how deeply valuable she was. In some ways, what I didn't want was for her to be too much like *I* was as a girl. Too often I shrank in the face of conflict. (I still battle this tendency.) I spoke too quietly. I smiled and said everything was all right, even when it absolutely was not. Pregnant with the baby who would burst into the world as my Isabel, I held the flimsy paper and stared at the ultrasound images of my little daughter growing inside of me and prayed that she would be strong.

I don't know whether it was my prayers, the genetic roll of the dice, God's providence, or a combination of all three, but from birth, my daughter Isabel has been a force to be reckoned with. She *is* smart, confident, and strong—and she is, truly, more than I could have ever hoped that my daughter would be. (Remember: I'm happy to shout it from the mountaintops: I adore all of my children. I'm smitten. Besotted. For more, see the introduction to this book.)

On Thanksgiving this year, my husband, our kids, and I made a fire in the fireplace and took turns naming something about someone else in the family for which we were most thankful. My younger daughter, Mia, has recently been enamored with sprinkling big words into conversation. She said she was thankful that one of her brothers is "unique" and "compassionate." Of the other, she said he was "humorous" and "exceptional." Of her sister, she said she is "courageous" and "perceptive." When it was my husband David's turn to say what he most loved about Isabel, he pulled her closer to him on the couch.

"I love how you care for people. People who are . . ." He was quiet a moment, searching for the right word.

"On the margins," Theo said, finishing his sentence.

"In some kind of need," I suggested at the same moment as Theo spoke.

"Yes," David agreed. "I am thankful for the way you help people who are on the margins or in need."

"Not on the margins," Isabel insisted. "*Different*. When you see a big group of people, it's like everyone's wearing black. But there are always a few people who have on, like, neon yellow. They're just different from everyone else. And I like being around the people who are different. Wearing the yellow. They're more interesting."

Which brings us back to the clementine oranges.

That day, after I asked about the missing oranges and

after Isabel held up that pencil and leveled her stare at me, the moment passed. It was probably because—although I'm generally not in favor of children bossing their parents around—I could tell whatever she was referring to was important, and I trust her. I've come to know that perfect submission from my kids isn't my goal as a mother.

What's even most likely is that before I could inquire about it further, something distracted me. Maybe Mia accidentally knocked a glass to the floor, and it shattered. Maybe one of the boys ran through the house with drippy, muddy snow on his boots. Maybe the dog scratched on the back door, pleading to come in. Maybe the phone rang, the kettle whistled, or the doorbell rang. Our home is an abundant source of distractions, and whatever was the particular one in that moment, I forgot about the missing clementines.

(This, by the way, is one argument in favor of having bigger families. You just don't have the time to fret over each and every thing your child says, does, or feels. Things pass. Fall between the cracks. Get forgotten. And that's okay.)

Over the next few weeks, I noticed the clementines' continued rapid depletion. The same was true for the baby carrots, apples, and other fruits and vegetables. I hoped (against hope) that the kids were finally seeing the light and deciding to snack on fresh produce when they were hungry. I soon learned that this wasn't the case.

A woman I knew helped out in the elementary school lunchroom. One day when I was volunteering at the school making photocopies in the teacher workroom, this friend came in and chatted with me.

"I just love your Isabel," she said. "I've been watching her in the lunchroom."

"Thank you! I love her too!" Her comment made my day. Who doesn't enjoy hearing that another adult appreciates your child?

"You know there's a new group of refugees here," she said. "Burmese. They grew up in Thai refugee camps."

"Oh," I said. The kids' school boasted kids from all over the world—and now Burma! "That's great."

"Yes, and your Isabel created a bit of a commotion with the lunch ladies about them. But I guess you heard all about that," she said.

"What?" I was ripped out of a daydream. I had been imagining what the Burmese kids thought of the snow, the playground, and the kids at their school in the Midwest after being born and raised in a refugee camp in Southeast Asia.

"I don't know anything about it," I said.

Isabel was making trouble with the lunch ladies? What next? Was she going to spray graffiti on the side of the school? My mind raced.

"The Burmese kids receive school lunches, but they've never seen the kinds of foods that are served. Apparently every day, they were just sitting there at lunch, staring at the microwaved pizza or pancakes. They didn't know what anything was or how to eat it. Isabel started sharing her lunch with them and one day I saw her bring a whole bag of oranges for them. I figured you'd given it to her to share."

"I had no idea about any of this," I said, suddenly remembering the missing clementines.

"One day there were chicken nuggets for hot lunch, shaped like dinosaurs I think, and Isabel just exploded. She got up from the table—which isn't allowed, by the way—and went into the kitchen. She stood in the doorway, her hands on her hips, and confronted the lunch ladies. 'Don't you have anything fresh in here? What's in that fridge? These kids are from Burma, and they don't eat chicken nuggets in Burma. They are hungry, for crying out loud. Can't you get them any *real* food? Something *fresh*?'"

I remembered Isabel's fiery glare when I asked her about the clementines. "I just need them. And we are not going to talk about it."

"So what happened?" I asked my friend.

"Oh, they told her to sit back down. Kids aren't allowed in the kitchen. But I heard about it. The other assistants and I think she's great."

I don't know whether her little outburst resulted in different food being given to the Burmese kids, but I was proud of her. I was also glad I'd not pressed her to tell me about what she'd done with the oranges. When I asked her about it, she just shrugged. "They were hungry. They couldn't figure out what the lunch ladies were giving them."

"What do they eat now?" I asked.

"Oh, I think they've gotten used to it. But when I go to their houses, I can tell they don't eat American food. There's always a rice cooker on the counter. And piles of fresh vegetables. The whole apartment smells good. Like a Chinese restaurant."

The case of the missing clementines was a lesson to me. It reminded me that my kids had their own lives and their own moral compasses. My strong, caring girl chose to help others, all on her own. I'm delighted to stand back and watch as she looks out for those "people wearing neon yellow" in so many environments. Proverbs 22:6 says, "Direct your children onto the right path, and when they are older, they will not leave it" (NLT). I like the gentle feel of that translation of the verse. *Direct your children.* I hope my husband and I have helped to *direct* Isabel toward looking out for others, but I know I can't claim the credit for her good works or good heart. The missing clementines gave me insight into who she is and into the fact that God is working within her to create a strong woman, beautiful in her love for others.

The softball season had just, unceremoniously, ended. Isabel's team had performed well all season and were contenders in the championship, but on that autumn day they were outplayed and lost the game. After Isabel and her teammates accepted their second-place trophies, David and I waited as the coach addressed them. I knew how much time the coach had put into developing his team. Of course he had wanted to win first place; all the coaches and players did. I didn't know the man well and wasn't sure how he'd respond to this end-of-season loss. He'd been gentle and affirming to the girls all season, but they'd made it into the championship. How would he treat them now that they had lost? I moved a little closer to the equipment box where he stood. Would he yell at his team? Would he call them out on errors they made? Who *was* this guy going to prove himself to be?

As I listened to his postseason speech, I was relieved that not only was he not going to *damage* the self-esteem of Isabel and the other girls on the team, he was communicating a number of valuable things to them. He asked each girl to share her favorite memory of the season. The girls wrote their thoughts on slips of paper and handed them to the coach. He then read them, one by one, and was delighted to find that every single player had written that her favorite moment was when one of the girls hit a grand slam in an important game. The girl who had accomplished this feat just grinned.

The coach had a bit of the St. Crispin's Day vibe going as he told them how proud he was of them. He said that the way they encouraged each other, worked hard, and treated their opposing teams with respect mattered far more to him than if they had won the championship game that day.

I leaned over to David.

"It takes a village," I whispered.

"Absolutely," he said.

A few weeks before that championship game, during one of the regular season games, another parent approached me.

"Did you hear?" he asked.

"I don't think so. What's wrong?"

"A kid from the high school killed himself today. I don't have details, but it's just so sad."

We stood in silence, watching our daughters take their positions in the field. I thought about all the love that this child had received in his life. I wondered how his parents would survive this loss. How would I?

Ian walked up behind me and stood beside us.

"What's going on? What's wrong?" he asked.

"Someone—a high schooler—killed himself today."

"Why? Why did he do it?" Ian asked.

The three of us stood quietly.

"I don't have any details," Isabel's teammate's father said. "I don't know."

"He must have felt he was all alone," I said.

"Yeah," Ian agreed. "I bet he did."

A few minutes later, my son and I walked across the park to the concession stand.

"Ian," I said. "You know you have people, right?"

"What? What do you mean?"

"Like, if you were ever feeling really isolated, you would have lots of people you could talk to. Not just Mom and Dad. You know that, right?"

"Are you worried that I'm depressed or something?" he asked.

"No. I'm just upset about that boy's death today. And I just want to make sure you know you're not alone."

"I know that, Mom. I've got lots of people," he said, giving me a little squeeze.

One of my goals since becoming a mother has been to make sure that my children's lives are rich with interaction with other trusted adults. I have always wanted my kids to know my friends well so that when, inevitably, there are times when my children can't call on David and me, they can approach other adults for help. These adults could hear confessions that might upset my husband and me. Such friends could give good counsel, serve as neutral voices, and offer friendship and support to my kids in tough times.

"Tell me a few of the other adults who love you," I asked.

Mr. "On the Bwight Side" met my gaze. He could tell I was upset. I saw his mood change from irritation to empathy. The tone of his voice softened. "Uncle Jimmy. Mark and Mary. David Fletcher," Ian answered. "Remember what David just did for me?"

He was referring to an experience a few weeks before when, at the tender age of thirteen, he had his first crisis of faith. One night after I tucked the girls into bed, I went in to check on Ian. He often reads the Bible right before turning off the light, and when I opened his door, he was sitting up reading.

"Say your prayers," I said, as I always do. "Oh, and please remember to pray for Isabel. I think she's coming down with pneumonia like she did a few years ago. I hear something wheezy in her chest and I'm taking her to the doctor tomorrow morning."

"Okay, will do!" Ian said.

A few minutes later, I was lying on my bed reading when Ian burst into the room. He had tears on his face.

"What's wrong?" I asked. "What happened?"

"You know you said to pray for Isabel? Just a minute ago? About her maybe having pneumonia? Well, I did. But as I prayed, I felt like there really wasn't a God. Like my prayers were just thoughts, just going around in my head and hitting up against the ceiling. I started praying harder, but I still felt that way."

By that point, he had crawled up beside me. I put my arm around him. "I've felt that way too, honey. At many different times in my life. It's a terrible feeling—it makes you feel so alone. But it doesn't mean that God's not there."

"I hate feeling this way. I would hate it if it were true."

Lying on my bed, I read him a few psalms.

"In the Bible, David went through times of doubt, times he was sure God had deserted him too," I said. "Times when he wasn't even sure God cared about him, or even existed."

"The psalms help," Ian said. "But would you do something for me?"

"Sure. Whatever you want," I said.

"Call David Fletcher. Tell him what's going on," Ian said.

David Fletcher, a former college professor of mine, has been a friend of our family for years. We attend the same church. We were, for several years, part of a small group. He not only serves as a fantastic Saint Nicholas every year at a children's luncheon at our church and is a respected professor of philosophy at my alma mater, but he has also befriended my kids since they were tiny. When my kids were very young, we'd have dinner with David and his wife, Joyce, and, inevitably, he'd run down to the basement and bring up a bin of Star Wars toys and play with my kids. They know him, and they trust him.

"Tell David I need advice about this," Ian said. "He's a philosopher, you know."

I tucked Ian back into bed, e-mailed David, and waited. I knew he would respond quickly if he was anywhere near his computer or smartphone. In a few minutes I received an e-mail in which he promised Ian that doubt was a normal, although terribly painful, part of faith. He assured Ian that God loves him and that our feelings about any relationship, whether with friends or with the Divine, can fluctuate. He told him he would pray for him. I printed out the e-mail and went to Ian's room. He was already sleeping, so I placed it on his bedside table.

I then e-mailed a few of my women friends, telling them about the pain Ian was in.

"That stinks," one said. "I get it and wish none of us—especially kids—ever had to experience it."

Another wrote back and said she would also pray for him.

In the morning, on waking, Ian found David's e-mail on his bedside table.

"How do you feel today?" I asked him at breakfast. "Any better?"

I told my son that I'd asked my girlfriends to pray for him and that they had.

"I feel better," Ian said. "And David's e-mail helped me. A lot. I guess it's kind of a big thing to keep choosing to believe. Thanks for reading those psalms to me last night. And thanks, most of all, for calling in my posse."

My posse.

It's a relief to me to remind myself that my kids' spiritual lives aren't up to me. God works in and through them, and when times get tough, they know to call in their posse. Or to steal all the clementines.

Yep, it takes a village.

CHAPTER 14

Old Mom, New Tricks
Adventures in Shape-Shifting

I might have mentioned I'm not very sporty, although it's true that I was on the basketball team in high school. That was because my brothers had played and I thought that's just what one did in high school. I wasn't much good, though, and eventually stopped playing. Happily, the shooting skills that have remained with me allow me to impress my children with an occasionally impressive shot during a game of H-O-R-S-E on our driveway. Additionally, my lack of knowledge about football has become something of a family joke. I'm improving, though. I recently learned that whole "four downs" thing. The same night I was taught that important component of the game, I was reminded that when I said "flashbacks," what I really meant was "replays." But for a brief time in my mothering, I was a bona fide Sporty Mom.

Because he had expressed interest in playing baseball since he was about ten months old, when Theo was five and finally old enough for a park district team, I signed him up. Some weeks later, I received a phone call. The caller identified himself as the commissioner of baseball (*the commissioner!*) and said that the park district had run into a small problem. They didn't have enough managers for the younger kids' teams, he explained, and he was hoping I would be willing to volunteer.

Manager! I pictured myself with the roster of players neatly attached to my clipboard. I saw myself handing out uniforms, filling large coolers with ice water, and maybe even organizing a team picnic at the end of the season. I would get to know the boys, be positioned to steer Theo toward or away from certain boys based on my observations. (Any kindergartners who chewed tobacco, for instance, would be off-limits to him for playdates.) Baseball manager—me! This would set me off on a path of being a supportive, involved mother to my firstborn child. I was ready and willing . . . and I even had reason to hope that they would give me a hat.

"I'd love to!" I said.

"Wonderful—that is such a *huge* help," he said. "And you can pick up the equipment any night next week."

"Gotcha!" I said. I wondered if the people at the park

district had heard that I was good with children as well as being organized. Later, of course, I would learn that they were just plain desperate and had asked each and every parent they'd called if he or she was willing to serve as the team's manager. (Um, I'd not, actually, been singled out for my temperament and/or unique skills.)

That night when David came home from work, I told him the good news.

"Guess what? I'm going to manage Theo's baseball team!"

"You're going to *what*?" David was incredulous.

"The commissioner of baseball called today. He asked me to be the manager. We're the Padres!" I said. "Look, I found this logo online. I made these stickers and am going to give them to the boys at the first practice."

"Jennifer," my husband said.

I stopped smiling. It's usually bad news when he calls me by my full name.

"Do you know what a baseball *manager* is?"

"Yes, of course I do. Look, I know we're busy, honey, but they didn't have enough managers. We'd have to drive him to practices anyway. How much trouble could it be?"

"In baseball, *manager* is another word for *coach*," he said.

"Are you sure?" I asked, nearly whispering.

"I can't believe you agreed to do it. You know *nothing* about baseball. You'll have to call whoever it is back and tell him you can't do it."

I found his tone patronizing. Now I was irritated.

"Um, *hello*," I said. "I have a *master's degree*, I think I can figure out how to coach baseball to five-year-olds."

"You have a master's degree in *English*!" he said. "It's not like they're going to read *Beowulf*. You know *nothing* about the game—how can you coach it?"

"I'll figure it out," I said. "Anyway, how do *you* know what I do or do not know about baseball? Drew and I used to listen to the Cubs on the radio. *All the time*. Billy Williams! José Cardenal! I remember them all."

"No, you don't," David said.

"And may I remind you that I was on my high school basketball team?"

"I just can't believe it," David said, slapping his hand to his forehead.

For the next week, I read what I could about baseball. I enlisted a friend who had coached his son's team to teach me to throw. We stood in his backyard and broke in my brand-new glove. He showed me how to move toward the ball and to use both hands to catch the ball. My friend gave me photocopies of all the drills, memos, and other paperwork he used when he coached little boys' teams. I asked my baseball-crazy father-in-law if he would be my assistant. Happily the prospect of spending time with his grandson persuaded him to do it.

I was delighted and greatly relieved. And, by the way, we all got free hats!

By the time practices started, I had a small, workable baseball vocabulary. When the team showed up on the first day of practice, some without knowledge of which base to run to after hitting the ball off of the tee, I realized the Padres and I would be just fine. I knew how to say "protect the plate" and "choke up on the bat." I made a very attractive snack schedule, I printed out those adorable Padres stickers, and, yes, I even organized an end-of-season picnic. (My husband and father-in-law helped. A lot.)

Coaching the Padres wasn't the first or last time I blindly jumped into some aspect of being a mom. (It was, however, the last time I coached a sports team. The next year, my husband and his father returned as Theo's coaches. I was in charge of snacks and keeping track of the checks and forms on picture day.)

Being a parent means trying on new (baseball) hats from time to time. It means taking risks and finding yourself in unfamiliar situations. It means doing what you can so your child can be on a baseball team, even if that means coaching a sport about which you know very little. It means using phrases you never thought you'd say, such as "Choke up on that bat" or, in other parts of my life, "Don't lick the dog's mouth" or, "Public bathrooms are no laughing matter."

I'm not saying we should all volunteer to do things we know nothing about, but I've seen parents bloom in beautiful ways when they try new things on behalf of their children.

Teaching art appreciation. Helping with a vacation Bible school program. Taking martial arts. Taking a course at a nature center about bats. Learning about a particular animal or insect. Learning to bake cupcakes from scratch. Jumping in, rebooting our interests, and taking risks are some of the fringe benefits of being a parent.

It's all good, right?

I answered the phone; it was a priest at my church.

"I wonder if you would help me with something," she said. "It's for the moms' group."

I froze. I'd been taking a deliberate hiatus from volunteering at church after a few years of doing far too much and wearing way too many hats. My life as a church volunteer had gotten to the point that on Sunday mornings I felt like I was going to work. I'd pack a bag with files, photocopies, and materials. I'd make a list of all the people I needed to speak to before they disappeared into their regular lives for the week. I edited the church newsletter, was director of the vacation Bible school program, and performed other children's ministry roles such as running background checks on nursery volunteers and other people who had contact with children in the church. (This last task, by the way, was highly satisfying to my Harriet-the-Spy-self.)

But, somewhere along the line, I had become Church Volunteer Mom. In some ways, it felt like I didn't have any other choice. After all, if a person has four children enrolled in Sunday school and is taking advantage of church programs, shouldn't she be involved in keeping them running?

Also, our church had suffered a painful split and those of us who stayed—"The Remnant," as we called ourselves then—had to buck up and cover the bases. A friend, Trey, dealt with the church split with humor. As I'd walk through the nearly abandoned nave after church, a thick stack of file folders under my arm and my hands closed around a giant carton of goldfish crackers, Trey would shout to me, David Letterman style, "Top Ten Best Things about the Split!"

"Number ten!" he called, as I pushed through the heavy door to the Sunday school rooms. "You'll always find a parking spot right next to the church!"

My friends—including Trey—and I did "buck up" and increase our pledges, ratchet up our participation, and "hold down the fort" in those lonely early days of what we called "The Troubles." Like many of my friends, I decided that I would do everything in my power to support the church and its work . . . even though I knew I was burning out. The problem with that line of thinking was that, after several months, church no longer was a place where I was quiet and found space to connect with God after a busy week with my kids. Church became (another) part-time job.

"It's a small thing," my priest said, sensing my reticence to her request for help. "Just one evening out, but mostly just developing a friendship with another mom."

"Well, okay," I said. "I think I can do it."

"Great—the deal is, we are trying to connect young moms and old moms," she said. My mind went to some of the senior women at my church, their wise smiles and kind hearts. Some of my richest friendships over the years have been with women of earlier generations than my own. After the split, an octogenarian named Wilma became my friend. Maybe I'd be paired with her, I hoped.

At position number one of my "Top Ten Best Things about the Split" was the deep friendships I'd made with older women in the church during The Troubles. I went from socializing mostly with young moms like myself to sitting in the gentle and nurturing presence of seniors. My kids got to know people in their eighties and nineties. At coffee hour, the young/old segregation no longer worked. There just weren't enough people in the room to accommodate such a division. We were all together and the wisdom, humor, and life experiences that the older folks shared with us in that painful time calmed and grounded my family and me.

"Old moms and young moms—yes. That's a great idea!" My curiosity was piqued.

"I'm pairing women up. To give each other support, in our mothering," she said.

"Wonderful!" I said.

"So I have a young mom, she's fairly new to the church, whom I'd like to assign to you," my priest said.

"So, I'd be the . . ."

"Old mom. Old*er*. I mean, the *experienced* mom," she said. "You know, you'd be available to talk to her when she's having a hard time. Her kids are younger than yours. You might be able to offer her guidance sometimes. Or just be her friend."

After I'd swallowed my surprise (and pride) and accepted that I was "the old mom," I completed the first task of the assignment. It was to send my "young mom" a note in the mail. Just a little introduction and a promise that I'd be praying for her and was available whenever she would like to chat.

I recommend this to other women. Pick a neighbor or woman at your church and send her a friendly note. If you can't figure out who to send it to, look to the last pew of your church, toward the house on your street with the orange cones across the end of the driveway, or at the woman who forgot to brush the back of her hair and has the crusty spit-up on her shoulder. She can use a kind word and your prayers. (Trust me!)

Just having an "old mom" to talk to seemed like a comfort to the mom to whom I was assigned. I'd see her outside of the church and say hello, as I'd done several times over the months since I met her, but now instead of just smiling politely and saying hi, she would tell me what was *really* going on for her. Concerns about one child's academic progress. Her husband's busy work life. Her difficulties balancing career and family. Her youngest child's refusal to use a potty.

"I don't know what I'm doing," she would say, shaking her head. (How many times have you thought, or said, those words? I couldn't begin to answer for myself. *Infinity* times?) Mostly, I just listened to her, but I also said what I knew to be true and what I most longed to hear when my children were really small:

"You're doing great. And it gets easier. I promise."

I take an online quiz that promises to tell me what kind of mom I am.

What's it going to be? *Sporty Mom? Church Volunteer Mom? TV-Free Mom? Old Mom?* Even though I eschew labels, I still wonder what the quiz will tell me about what kind of mom I "really" am.

I answer the questions quickly and, after my score is tabulated, I learn that my "Mommy Style" is . . . drum roll, please . . . Earthy Mom! Yay! Remember the soymilk and organic baby food at the grocery store? I think I was tagged as "earthy" because I admitted that my family is serious about recycling, that I chose the sling as the best way to carry an infant, and because I preferred "I Got You, Babe" to Madonna's "Vogue" or Chaka Khan's "I'm Every Woman" as my "Mom Theme Song." (Just FYI—the Beatles' "With a Little Help from My Friends" wasn't an option.)

I got zero percent as my Sporty Mom score. (Zero! This after I coached the Padres? So what do *they* know?) My Fashionista Mom score was dismally low. I got a fairly good score for Classic Mom, but far fewer points than I'd expect for Multitasking Mom. (That last score offended me a bit. I grant you that I'm not a fashionista or really very sporty. But a multitasker? I failed on *that*? Have you seen me at dinnertime? I'm like one of those people who can spin plates. Homework! Phone calls! Permission slips! Butternut squash and coconut milk soup! Neighbor kids ringing the doorbell to sell popcorn and Girl Scout cookies! I can manage it all—and all at once!)

Oh well. I'll take the Earthy Mom moniker. After all, I've been called all sorts of things as a mom. Weeks after Theo was born, a friend asked me what we'd decided regarding circumcision. She also had a newborn son and, like me, was a first-time mother consumed by learning to care properly for her infant. Without violating my son's privacy, let's just say that the doctors at my practice were old-school about the matter. They assured us that it was up to us whether to have our newborn sons circumcised, but, they cautioned, "it's a lot more painful and it can be really embarrassing when they're older." When I told my friend what decision we had made, she was outraged on Theo's behalf.

"The poor lamb. I would like you to know I think that is the most brutal thing I've ever heard," she said. "I never took you for such a *barbarian*."

Oops.

Barbarian Mom.

I wasn't deterred. The deed, so to speak, had been done and I felt content that we'd made an informed choice. If you'd been in the room with me when my ob/gyn told the story of recently circumcising a teenage boy after he'd suffered a series of infections, your toes would have curled. Seriously.

A few months later, the same friend called to ask how (the poor lamb) Theo was sleeping.

"It's going great," I said. "He's sleeping through the night. Ever since we Ferberized him."

"You *what?*"

"You know, Ferberized him. It's a method that teaches babies to settle themselves and to go to sleep on their own. You let them cry it out, but just incrementally. You know, you put them in the crib, leave the room, and then come in and give them a pat or talk to them at longer and longer intervals until they learn to get to sleep on their own. It took three nights, but now he sleeps like a champ."

"You let a six-month-old 'cry it out'?" she asked.

"The longest he cried was about twenty minutes. Which he was doing anyway," I said. I didn't tell her how I'd cried too, sitting on the floor in the hall outside of his room. But, after those three nights, he never had sleep issues again.

"I don't care what you call it, that's just cruel," she said.

Cruel Mom.

Again, I was unperturbed by my friend's dismay. I saw what a happy, well-adjusted baby Theo was, and I knew how desperately I needed to sleep at night myself. After he started sleeping through the night, I started to feel like a human being again. About a year later, the same woman called and asked me another parenting question. I don't recall whether she was inquiring about breastfeeding or a teething issue, but whatever it was, I had the distinct sense that we'd again be on different sides of the fence when I shared my approach with her.

"Do you really want to talk about this?" I asked. "I mean, in the past we've approached things, um, rather differently. I don't want to upset or offend you."

"Look," she said. "I don't care if you say you hang your baby from his toes in the attic. I'm losing my mind over here. I get no sleep and I'm drained and I just don't know what to do. You've got to talk to me. *Now*!"

A year of caring for an infant had rubbed off some of her rough patches. I realized that she had changed. Radically. I was relieved to no longer be Barbarian Mom or Cruel Mom, but rather a friend who was invited to dispense honest advice. Like me, this woman was just doing her best in a culture that puts unfair pressure on mothers to do everything exactly right. And, like me, she learned to relax over the years.

We'll all do it differently. A Helicopter Mom will measure the temperature when she draws her baby's bath. A Tiger Mother will follow her convictions about parenting and draw battle lines with her kids. A Hippie Mama will draw unicorns. I say, draw on all the pieces of who God made you to be in your mothering. Your faith, your friends, and your special gifts and insights. Acknowledge your best and worst selves and give love, boundaries, and grace to your children as you raise them. Try to make time to eat together. Play together. Unplug sometimes. These things help us connect with our children.

I may not know the right answers on many parenting issues, but I am convinced that being *connected* to our children, accepting and loving them as the unique and worthwhile people they are, covers a multitude of parenting sins. Being connected with them sets our kids up—as much as possible—for a life of healthy connection with others and with the God who created them and who is even more smitten with them than we are.

CHAPTER 15

Hide and Seek
Adventures in Being Present

They run through the house, pound up the stairs, and fold themselves into closets and under beds. How many kids are here? I don't know exactly. It's my four children and some of their friends. Fewer than ten, I'm guessing. Some live in the neighborhood and sort of come and go on these summer afternoons.

The child who has been charged with counting from one to one hundred begins to tire of the task at about the number fifty. They all have started petering out about then, skipping more and more numbers. He speeds up and skims through: "49. 52. 58. 60. 65. 70. 87. 100!" When he finally calls out "Ready or not, here I come!" all of the others, crouched on the floor of the pantry, breathing hard under a bed, or standing very still behind the living room curtains, fall silent. After a few minutes, Mia slides open the shower door and creeps over to me in my bedroom.

"I *kill* at this," she whispers. "I've been in there *forever*." She sneaks back into the bathroom and I hear her slide the shower door closed again. My brain does one of its split-screen—and admittedly slightly neurotic—reactions and, all at once, I wonder about the expression she's used. *Kill at this*? What would Michael Moore say? Is this some sign of a more violent society? That "killing" at something is the cool thing to say? The expression a little girl will say when she is proud of herself? I then weigh the relative merits of adding that expression to my vocabulary. Could I pull it off, at forty-four and living here in the suburbs? *I kill at this*? Would that be sort of hip? At exactly the same moment, I wonder if the shower floor is wet and whether there will be muddy flip-flop footprints in the shower and on the bathroom floor. Next I remember that some of the kids came in the side gate earlier. I hope they closed it so we won't have to go on a hunt to find the dog later on this afternoon. My brain is full to overflowing and moves fast over all of these matters as my daughter tries to suppress her giggles in the shower. *Okay, stop it, stop it, stop it.* I try to silence my mind. I breathe in, I breathe out. I look out the window into the front yard.

A little while later, all the kids have been found or have grown bored with waiting to be discovered and have revealed themselves by bursting out of hiding places and shouting to each other.

"No one even came in the room!"

"Ha! You walked right past me!"

"I was there, all along! Behind the curtain!"

They're delighted with themselves. They abandon the game of hide-and-seek and move *en masse* out onto the back porch. It's the end of July and the pale blue sky keeps closing over with dark clouds and then opening up again. It can't make up its mind about whether to storm. The kids play outside and when a few raindrops fall, they come inside, only to run back out again a few minutes later. I watch from the window as they drop rubber bases onto the grass and start negotiations for a game of baseball. My youngest, Mia, opts out of playing the game and walks to a swing, knowing full well that her siblings will cajole her into being on one of the teams. They run after her, and one of her brothers even falls to his knees in a mock posture of begging. In a few moments she joins the game, pleased with herself. Her brothers and sister exchange smiles; they're willing to play her game so that she will play theirs.

This scene, so completely normal and unspectacular, is my happy ending. A home in the suburbs, a pack of happy children, and a houseful of hiding places. I'm thankful that there are no secrets lurking in those closets, no questions or confusing conversations to silence them. They can slip under the beds in a game of hide-and-seek or crouch behind the garbage cans in the garage and not find anything that will shock or confuse them. It's the (emotional) gold at the end of the rainbow for me, an afternoon like this. It's that Velveteen love of raising kids with all the fledge words and fairy dust, yesses and nos and snuggles on the couch and sleepless nights that parenting entails.

I take a deep breath and my mind flashes on a familiar image. It is the last scene of *Raising Arizona*, a movie I've watched probably a dozen times. I sometimes put it on just for the payoff of the last scene when H. I. narrates his prophetic dream. Nicholas Cage plays H. I. McDunnough, an ex-con and a recidivist or "ree-peat oh-fender" as his parole board describes him. With his wife Ed (from Edwina), H. I. wants nothing more than to have a baby and to share all the love and beauty in the world with that child.

I won't spoil the movie for you—a strange and delightfully bizarre one—but the final scene reveals a sleeping H. I.'s dream about family. He sees his wife and himself, fast-forwarded in time to when they are seniors and sit around a dinner table with their grown children and grandkids as they break bread together. He describes the setting of the dream as a kind of heaven where parents are "wise and capable" and children are "happy and beloved."

What more could we wish for as parents but these things?

Family—being a wife to David and being my children's mother—isn't all I've ever wanted in life. I desire true, intimate friendships. I want to continue to grow in my craft as a writer. I want to deepen spiritually. But being a wife and mother is indeed something I've hoped for as long as I can remember, and I savor the gifts of family. I want ours to be a family who works to make the world a better place. I want to raise children who can walk into adulthood as unencumbered as possible. I don't want them to be mired in bad memories, looking back at their family of origin in confusion, with regret, or having to work hard to make sense of what they have experienced as children. I want my children to be free. I want David and me to be wise and capable parents. I want ours to be happy and beloved children. At least *most of the time.* That's what I hope for. And, so far, like H. I. in his dream, I think I'm managing to create something, with God's help, that is good.

And I hope the same for you too.

CONCLUSION

The Dollhouse
Adventures in Letting Go

Only a few remnants of the dollhouse remained. The father figure with his porcelain face, blue shirt, and wide-legged khaki pants. The wooden dining table, the size of a paperback book. Two plates from the set of dishes. The baby with her cloth face and tiny silk pajamas. A rolltop desk. A bathtub with a tiny metal faucet. A stamp-sized throw cushion.

For decades, these relics lived in a cardboard box in my basement, near the water heater, the bin of giftwrap and ribbons, and boxes of Christmas decorations. The box was loaded into and out of moving trucks half a dozen times over the years, its corners ever more crushed, the paper fibers weakening from being pressed for too long into dank corners.

The dollhouse was given away years ago when I was in college. When I realized it was gone, despite being a young adult, light-headed over new love and pleased with my rag-tag group of friends and thrift-store couture—fake pearls, T-shirts, men's blazers, and ankle-length skirts—I mourned its loss.

About five feet long and three feet high, with a yellow roof made of corrugated plastic, my dollhouse had real car-pet on the floors and wallpapered walls. Open at the front, three deep drawers along its base served as storage, the house's basement. Someone—I don't remember who—had built the dollhouse for a child who didn't care for it. It was given to our family when I was too young to notice it being brought into the house.

To say that I found dusting the little shelves of the china cabinet or centering a potted plant on the kitchen window-sill to be satisfying tasks does not begin to speak to how much I loved playing with my dollhouse.

When I was a child I lived in what often felt like a very uncertain world, punctuated by my parents' failing marriage and the confusion of being the youngest child in a family that seemed to be spinning and swirling into and out of focus around me. That dollhouse was an island of calm. No doors slammed, no phones rang, and no secrets lurked in its shadows. There were just the five people who lived there, serenely moving through open doorways from the kitchen to the dining room to the family room upstairs. And only I touched it, arranged the furniture, sat the figures beside each other on the sofa or stood them shoulder-to-shoulder at the kitchen sink.

I'd kneel in front of my dollhouse for hours, carefully setting the table with plates and tiny silverware or gently pressing on the ends of the runners of the wooden rocking chair in the nursery where the mother sat. I blew dust off of the tea set, seated the family at the dinner table, and placed the tiny gray cat by the fireplace.

The whole house was completely under my control; its residents happily succumbed to my benevolent will for them. I longed for a home someday that was so beautifully ordered and for a family that so peacefully lived together.

When I noticed its absence and was told by my mother that she had given the dollhouse away some time earlier, I'm sure my grief was puzzling to her. It likely seemed disproportionate to the loss of that oversized wooden structure from my childhood.

I was glad to find that some of the dollhouse's contents— the desk, the dining table, a few dolls and dishes—had made their way into the back of a nearby closet and were left behind. I gathered them up and kept them in a box in my basement for decades.

That is, I kept them until a few months ago.

I don't know what made me do it—procrastination about getting to my desk and to work, probably—as I padded around the house. I'd just changed over the laundry when I turned and faced what I call "the deep, dark part" of my basement. The children were at school, David was at work, and the dog was lying outside in the sun. The house was quiet. I walked toward the workbench and the storage area with its shelves stacked with tools, old accordion files, and bins of winter coats and boots.

I waved my hand above my head and pulled on the light cord. The lone bulb halfheartedly lit up the space. There, beside a stack of rolled-up sleeping bags, was that old box. I pulled it down from the shelf, gave the chain another yank, and went upstairs to my kitchen, bright on a sunny autumn day.

I set the box on the table and opened the flaps. The dollhouse furniture that I found inside wasn't as pristine and beautiful as I remembered. Time and decay had done their work. The dining table was scratched and missing a leg. The pink gingham pillow was stained with age. Dots of mildew marred the wooden bathtub as though no one had scrubbed it for a long time. The rolltop desk lacked drawers. The father doll and baby were missing. Everything smelled musty and was covered in a sticky film of dust. As I tossed each piece back into that old box, the dirty, broken furniture made a hollow clatter.

Nothing was worth keeping.

I smiled at myself and wondered why I had been hanging on to those old, broken things for so long.

As a girl, I was always scraping my knees climbing trees or falling off of my skateboard. The skin is still tough after years of having been battered and bandaged. As a girl, sometimes I'd leave the bandage on so long, thinking the wound was probably just beginning to heal, that I was surprised when I pulled it off and a thick brown scab was just sort of hovering on top of my skin. I would realize that I'd lost track of how long I'd been wearing the bandage. The cut had already healed and no longer needed me to cover it over.

It was like that with the box of dollhouse stuff.

What had I been waiting for? Why'd I keep carting that box around for so long?

I carried the box out of the house into the garage and dropped it into a garbage can. Afterward, I stood on the back porch for a while. I picked up a few pieces of thick chalk the girls had left outside. They'd drawn their names on the concrete in letters two feet tall. *Isabel. Mia.* On the other side of the picnic table were the names of the rest of the family. *Theo. Ian. Dad. Mom.* Hearts were drawn around each one.

I watched the wind move through the trees in the backyard.

The limbs of our small pear tree leaned and strained as though the tree was poised to begin a race. Its leaves danced and turned; they seemed to be given over to wild applause.

APPENDIX 1
Five Multiple-Duty Products Busy Moms Shouldn't Be Without

G/MLS CHEERIOS	$4.49
POST-IT 4PK	$1.99
SHRP FINE 2 CT	$1.99
DGTL TMR	$4.00
GD CK CNTRS/50 CT	$10.00
TOTAL	**$22.97**

I've been a mother for more than sixteen years and, during that time, have bought, sold, lost, donated, and discarded hundreds—perhaps thousands—of dollars' worth of what I thought upon purchasing them would be lasting and vital tools for family life. These include but are not limited to parenting books, booster chairs, nursing pumps, and lava lamps.

But, looking back, there are five inexpensive items that have truly made my job as a mother simpler. They are cheap (get *all five* for less than twenty-five dollars), easy to find (drop by your neighborhood drugstore), and so useful that you'll find yourself reaching for them multiple times a day.

1. Permanent Markers
You can buy a basic two-pack of black fine-point Sharpies for a couple of dollars. And to move into Technicolor, spend

about ten dollars for a set of eight pens in various colors. (There are more than forty Sharpie colors, including "rain shower," "pink lemonade," and "clover." You've got to love the names, right?)

Once you tug the caps off, there's no end to the creative ways you will use them. (And, no, this is not a product placement. Much as I'd love Sharpie to give me some little perk for plugging their products, they have not.) Here are a few uses of your Sharpies/other permanent pens:

- **Label Your Children's Belongings**: These markers bring out the Picasso in many of us as we label— with artistic flourishes—our children's thermoses, brown bag or vinyl lunch bags, school supplies, bike helmets, and water bottles. Basic black can indelibly mark the clothing tags on your children's coats and sweatshirts. Mark baseball gloves, soccer balls, backpacks, and the insides of your children's shoes.

- **Teach Your Children Your Cell Phone Number**: If your child cannot remember your number, consider writing it neatly on the palm of his or her hand. I am not a person with tattoos myself and understand if you are offended by the idea of marking your child in this way, but staring at it will give him or her something to do when it's raining during kindergarten recess and the only other option is watching an episode of *SpongeBob*. (What *is* that starfish's name, anyway?)

- **Explore Your Inner Artist**: Have some fun with your Sharpies and make homemade construction-paper greeting cards. Or liven up your child's faint pencil drawings by tracing over them with an extra-fine-point Sharpie. Then ask your child to bring the work of art to life with watercolors. Watch over your kids when they are using Sharpies—they are, after all, *permanent.*

- **Get Your Home Organized**: Label basement storage bins, file boxes, shelves in the pantry, coat hooks, and the spine of three-ring binders with your markers. Organize and label stray DVDs of family photos and movies.

- **Make Yours Personal**: If you, like many at-home moms we know, become a bit . . . ahem . . . protective about your new permanent marker collection, you can even order personalized Sharpies from the company's website.

2. Kitchen Timers

Digital or old-fashioned turn-the-dial timers have multiple uses in a busy at-home mom's life. Because of the digital timers on your oven or microwave, you may not have ever considered buying one. But, perhaps now is the time and it will only cost about four dollars at your local grocery or drugstore.

- **Do Big Jobs in Several Small Chunks of Time:** If you have forty-five minutes before you need to leave to pick your children up from school or a playdate, set your timer for thirty-five minutes and begin a big job. Do a few pages of your scrapbook. File several documents that have been sitting on your desk for too long. Unpack one long-neglected box in your basement. Fold a load of laundry. When the timer goes off, you're done for now. The job may not be done all in one sitting, but that's okay. You might find another thirty-five minutes tomorrow.

- **Keep Children on Track:** Set the timer and give it to your children to use for piano practice. Prevent arguments by setting the timer before each child's turn at the video game system. Make a game of tasks like finding stray library books ("I'm setting the timer for five minutes—who can find the most books before the timer beeps?") or cleaning their rooms ("Who will have the neatest room before this buzzes?"). And, use it judiciously when your young child is sitting in time-out. (Just try not to hurt anyone's "booty," okay? See chapter 3, "Mommy Misdemeanors.")

- **Its Intended Purpose:** You can, of course, use your timer in the kitchen when you are making cakes or hard-boiled eggs!

3. Sticky Notes

These self-sticking notes as well as their price are appealing too. (You can buy generic ones as well as ones made from recycled paper.) A four-pack of about two hundred notes is around four dollars. You can leave notes to your children, sticking them to a lunch box or folder ("Piano lesson today" or "Remember Social Studies book" or "I love you so much!"), or attach notes to your husband's keychain or computer bag to remind him of a child's softball game or his mother's birthday.

Your children, as my daughter Isabel does, might take to sticking notes to the coffeemaker every night to remind you whether they have orchestra rehearsal or other early morning events the following day. You can also stick them to the television screen ("Homework and practice violin before TV!") or to the lid of the cookie jar ("Only two!"). Your life is chock-full of details. Using sticky notes helps your family attend to them—and even, amazingly, lets you feel like you are able to be in two places at once.

4. Reusable Plastic Containers

Back in the day, Tupperware was the only way to think about plastic containers—and indeed Tupperware can still wow us with their quality and array of colors, shapes, and sizes. (Their "Cake Taker," for instance, can be flipped over to transport deviled eggs. I mean, who knew?)

But these days, good plastic containers abound. You can find cheap plastic containers made by Glad and Good

Cooks, or even generic brands at dollar stores, drugstores, and most grocery stores. It's common to find a multipack of fifty or so containers for ten dollars or less, and they can be used for much more than cakes and deviled eggs.

- **Organize Art Supplies**: Use medium-sized containers to organize arts and craft supplies, separating crayons, markers, and stickers into separate bins.
- **Make Snacks**: Set up an assembly line on your kitchen counter and let your toddlers or older children prepare snack containers of pretzels, raisins, or dry cereal to be popped into your purse or the diaper bag.
- **Pack Waste-Free Lunches**: Be kind to the earth and trade plastic bags for reusable containers and pack sandwiches, chips, carrot sticks or cucumber slices, and cookies in them for your children's lunches.
- **Be Inventive**: These containers will be used over and over again . . . and if you lose a lid, store the bowl with your art supplies to hold water for your children when they paint. Older babies and young toddlers can stack them, play with them in the bathtub, and sort blocks and other small toys into them. When you're done with a container or lid, drop it into your recycling bin.

5. Cheerios

No list of double—or triple—use "mom friendly" products would be complete without . . . Cheerios! Generic "toasted oat rounds" work too—they are less expensive than the original, but even at four dollars a box, the real thing is still a bargain.

Cheerios:
- are often a child's first finger food.
- can be strung on yarn or glued to paper for easy art projects.
- can become part of a snack mix.
- can be used to teach a young child basic addition and subtraction.
- are guilt-free munchies for moms in the midst of an energy crash.
- make, of course, a great breakfast.

APPENDIX 2
Signs of Mommy Burnout

Even though you and all the other moms in the playgroup or at your office have dark circles under your eyes, *being exhausted is* not *a prerequisite for being a mom.* In fact, remaining in a perpetual state of exhaustion can undercut our best efforts to be loving mothers. Signs of mommy burnout include, but are not limited to, irritability and depression. Too often, overstressed parents lose—at least for a while—a sense of the larger picture of what they are doing and why they are choosing to do it. Raising children is important work, but after being up five nights in a row with sick children your patience and sense of humor can wear very thin or vaporize completely.

As your responsibilities at home increase, you may find yourself out of the habit of caring for yourself. You might get a false idea that taking care of your needs is the same as being selfish. And, with little ones counting on you for everything, the last thing you want to be is selfish.

But keep those flight safety instructions in mind and—when you find yourself snapping at your husband and kids or beginning to feel like your low mood won't lift—consider whether it's time to focus on caring for your own needs for a while.

WAYS TO REGAIN BALANCE

1. Remember what makes you happy

What little indulgences did you enjoy before you had children? If you skipped a class in college or took an afternoon off from work, what did you do? Did you watch your favorite movie for the tenth time? Did you peruse the library stacks? Did you get a massage? Take a bubble bath? If you found a twenty-dollar bill in your pocket in your pre-kid days, what did you spend it on? Chai tea? A bunch of Gerbera daisies? New Converse All-Stars? Scrapbooking supplies? A hip-hop CD? Don't wait for your husband to read your mind. Instead, choose to treat yourself with the quirky things that make you—and only you—happy.

2. Get out!

Sometimes after enduring bed rest and then the early months of nursing, some moms forget they can actually leave the house . . . as in, put on your actual shoes, open the front door, and walk right out the door.

Walking from the laundry room to the nursery to the kitchen and then back again day after day can make you feel trapped. But just getting outside can help you breathe easier and make you remember there is a whole universe outside your door.

Let your toddlers crouch on the sidewalk for five or ten minutes to study bugs. Kneel down beside them and see through their eyes for a few minutes.

- **Get yourself moving!** If you live in a place where leaves turn colors in the fall, go for a walk and collect the prettiest ones. Grab a soccer ball and take your child to a park or an empty field. Put your baby in the stroller and go for a brisk walk or a jog around the neighborhood. Regular exercise will improve your mood and will help you get a good night's sleep. (Two important benefits for busy moms.)
- Go **window shopping** with your kids at a local art gallery. Ask your children which painting they would buy if they had to choose just one.
- Even just **sitting outside** for ten minutes looking up at the expanse of sky can recharge a tired mom's batteries.

3. Know when enough is enough

It's an immense responsibility to raise a child—and no one does it perfectly. You might find yourself thinking that if your house and family doesn't look as picture-perfect as a 1950s television show you're falling short as a mother. Some moms put tremendous pressure on themselves to have flawlessly clean homes, eerily obedient children, and shatter-proof sunny dispositions. But, let's face it, none of us is Mary Poppins—real life is much messier than that. (And aren't we glad it is? All that singing and jumping through chalk paintings could get annoying.)

Embrace reality! It's okay if the clean clothes stay in the basket for a few days. It's not the end of the world if you serve spaghetti three times in one week. No one will be traumatized if your children run around the backyard in their bare feet and track muddy footprints into the house.

You don't have to do your job as a mother perfectly—in fact it's impossible to do so. Parenting is about real life. Your real life. And your real children need you to take good care of yourself—so strap that oxygen mask onto yourself first!

APPENDIX 3
A Prayer to Tear out of This Book

Almighty God, heavenly Father,
you have blessed us with the joy
and care of children: Give us calm
strength and patient wisdom as we bring them up,
that we may teach them to love
whatever is just and true and good,
following your example of our Savior Jesus Christ.
Amen.

(*Book of Common Prayer*, 829)

Acknowledgments

Singer Bruce Cockburn wrote, "To be held in the heart of a friend is to be a king."[1] I am grateful to have friends who make me feel like royalty. Special thanks to Tricia and Michael Benich, Suzanne Ecklund, Keiko and Rob Feldman, Sara Hendren and Brian Funck, Mary and Mark Lewis, Catharine Phillips, Cathleen Falsani and Maurice Possley, Caryn Dahlstrand Rivadeneira, (Uncle) Jimmy Saba, Susan and Scott Shorney, Jenny and Eric Sheffer-Stevens, Thad Smith, and the Treahouses. I'm hugely grateful for our intimate and abiding friendships.

Special thanks to Kathy and Jeremy Treat (and sons) for uncountable gifts and for letting me be the houseguest who wouldn't leave as I finished this book. Nick and Jake Reber—*hermanos*!—your humor, intelligence, and generosity never cease to amaze me. Thank you, Coy and Cooper Treat, for sharing your life and insights about the importance of family with me. Thank you, Cooper, for the illustrations you made and for letting me cuddle with Slushy and Loopy. (They were very comforting pets to a writer far from home.) Thank you, Oscar, for sitting on my feet while I wrote, even though it was quite naughty of you to jump on the kitchen table whenever Kathy and Jeremy weren't around. (Yeah, I warned you I'd tattle on you.)

Thank you to the founders and members of Redbud Writers Guild for your continued support and friendship. Check out these world-changers at redbudwriters.com.

Thank you, Margaret Feinberg and Dave Zimmerman, for the good advice you gave me when you attended Redbud regarding pages that would become part of this book.

Thank you, Claire Siemer, for your attentive and loving care of my children as you babysit, tutor, and take them to Starbucks when I'm working.

Thank you to other friends who inspire me with your humor, your creativity, and the difference you make in our world, including Kelly Allison (please thank Seth for the terrorist line—still makes me laugh), Beth Andersen, Amy Julia Becker, Felicia Bertch, Eileen Button, Maura and Paul Constance, Amy Hilbrich Davis, Carolyn Craig Ebner, Joyce and David Fletcher, Grace and Michael Freedman, Susan Maynor, Anthony Platipodis, Susan Schmalzbauer, James M. Smith, Margot Starbuck, Sarah Vanderveen, and Linda Wilkinson.

Thank you, Jennifer Ochs, for the PWTs and for surviving that mission trip van crash with me when we were in high school. (Our story!)

Thank you to Byron Williamson, Jeana Ledbetter, Kris Bearss, Sherrie Slopianka, Rob Birkhead, Alyson White, Morgan Canclini, and everyone at Worthy Publishing for your warmth and excellent support.

Thank you, once again, to Jennifer Haney Stair for your editing prowess.

Thanks to the members of The Thread for your friendship, prayers, and more than occasional brilliance.

Thank you to my priests, George Smith and Elizabeth Molitors.

Thank you, as ever, to my in-laws, Alethea and Larry Funck.

Thank you to my mother, Myrna Reid Grant, for your example of love and strength and also, yes, even for that powdered milk.

Thank you to my brothers, Chris and Drew Grant, and their Julies.

Thank you, last and certainly far from least, to my family. Huge thanks to my husband, David, for taking excellent care of our kids when I was off finishing this book and, as ever, for our life together. You are good and true. You are also infinitely patient with me and bring me coffee and I thank you for all of the above. Thank you to Theo, Ian, Isabel, and Mia for giving me permission to share these stories and for being generally delightful. I thank all of you for being on this messy but supremely charming adventure with me.

I'm smitten with you.

(But you know that.)

Notes

Introduction: Velveteen Parenting

1. Carla Barnhill, *The Myth of the Perfect Mother: Rethinking the Spirituality of Women* (Grand Rapids: Baker, 2004).

Chapter 1: Fledge Words and Fairy Dust

1. Po Bronson, "How Not to Helicopter," *Newsweek*, November 20, 2009; http://www.thedailybeast.com/newsweek/blogs /nurture-shock/2009/11/20/how-not-to-helicopter.html

2. E. E. Cummings, "i thank you God for most this amazing," *E. E. Cummings: Complete Poems, 1904-1962 (Revised Corrected, and Expanded Edition)*, ed. George James Firmage (New York: Liveright, 1994).

Chapter 3: Mommy Misdemeanors

1. See "The Story of Stuff Project" at http://www.storyofstuff. org/. See also Luke 12:33, "Sell your possessions and give to those in need. This will store up treasure for you in heaven!" (NLT).

2. Unconfirmed, but assumed to be fact.

3. "Bands complain about their songs being used in torture," *The Telegraph*, December 11, 2008; http://www.telegraph.co.uk/ news/worldnews/northamerica/usa/3705755/Bands-complain -about-their-songs-being-used-in-torture.html

Chapter 4: Escape to Gordon's House

1. Jennifer Grant, "The Charlie Sheen Has Worn Off," *Her.meneutics*, March 11, 2011; http://blog.christianitytoday .com/women/2011/03/the_charlie_sheen_has_worn_off.html

2. From a personal e-mail to author, September 2011. See also Hilbrich Davis' website, Familylifesuccess.com

Chapter 5: Behind the Amish

1. Cathleen Falsani, *Sin Boldly: A Field Guide for Grace* (Grand Rapids: Zondervan, 2008).

2. Ibid., 10.

3. "Modern life leads to more depression among children," *The Telegraph*, September 12, 2006; http://www.telegraph.co.uk/ news/1528639/Modern-life-leads-to-more-depression-among -children.html

4. Ben Fenton, "Junk culture 'is poisoning our children'," *The Telegraph*, September 12, 2006; http://www.telegraph.co.uk/news/1528642/Junk-culture-is-poisoning-our-children.html

5. Ibid.

6. Peter Gray, "The Dramatic Rise of Anxiety and Depression in Children and Adolescents: Is It Connected to the Decline in Play and Rise in Schooling?" January 26, 2010; http://www.psychologytoday.com/blog/freedom-learn/201001/the-dramatic-rise-anxiety-and-depression-in-children-and-adolescents-is-it

7. Esther Entin, "All Work and No Play: Why Your Kids Are More Anxious, Depressed," *Atlantic*, October 12, 2011; http://www.theatlantic.com/life/archive/2011/10/all-work-and-no-play-why-your-kids-are-more-anxious-depressed/246422/

8. See Flylady.net

9. Carla Barnhill, "Simplified Summer," June 6, 2011, *The Mommy Revolution* blog; http://themommyrevolution.wordpress.com/2011/06/06/simplified-summer/

10. Ibid.

11. Anish Kapoor, interview with John Tusa, BBC Radio; http://www.bbc.co.uk/radio3/johntusainterview/kapoor_transcript.shtml

Chapter 6: There's Something about Blue French Fries

1. Juliet B. Schor, "The Commodification of Childhood: Tales from the Advertising Front Lines," *The Hedgehog Review*, Summer 2003; http://www.iasc-culture.org/HHR_Archives/Commodification/5.2CSchor.pdf

2. Ibid.

3. http://www.webmd.com/add-adhd/guide/food-dye-adhd

4. Senate Committee on the Judiciary, "Children, violence, and the media: a report for parents and policy makers," September 14, 1999. Previously available at http://judiciary.senate.gov/oldsite/mediavio.htm

5. Internet Resources to Accompany *The Sourcebook for Teaching Science*, "Television and Health"; http://www.csun.edu/science/health/docs/tv&health.html#tv_stats

6. Ibid.

7. Rabbi Lawrence Kelemen, "The Dangers of TV," Simple to Remember;http://www.simpletoremember.com/articles/a/dangers-of-television/

8. Steven Dowshen, MD, "How TV Affects Your Child," Kids Health, October 2011; http://kidshealth.org/parent/positive/family/tv_affects_child.html#

9. Annie Leonard, *The Story of Stuff*, referenced and annotated script; http://dev.storyofstuff.org/wp-content/uploads/2011/10/annie_leonard_footnoted_script.pdf

10. Ibid.

11. http://currey-wilson.com/faq.php

12. "Reading Aloud to Kids: The 12 Benefits of Reading Books Out Loud to Children of All Ages," SixWise.com; http://www.sixwise.com/newsletters/07/02/07/reading-aloud-to-kids-the-12-benefits-of-reading-books-out-loud-to-children-of-all-ages.htm

13. Carson McCullers, *The Heart Is a Lonely Hunter* (New York: Bantam, 1983).

14. Isak Dinesen, *Out of Africa* (New York: Random House, 1938).

15. John Berendt, *Midnight in the Garden of Good and Evil* (New York: Random House, 1984).

Chapter 8: On the Bwight Side . . .

1. Po Bronson, "In Defense of Children Behaving Badly," *Newsweek*, October 22, 2009; http://www.thedailybeast.com/newsweek/blogs/nurture-shock/2009/10/22/in-defense-of-children-behaving-badly.html

2. Siegfried Engelmann, Phyllis Haddox, and Elaine Bruner, *Teach Your Child to Read in 100 Easy Lessons* (Clearwater, FL: Touchstone, 1986).

3. Po Bronson, "In Defense of Children Behaving Badly," *Newsweek*, October 22, 2009; http://www.thedailybeast.com/newsweek/blogs/nurture-shock/2009/10/22/in-defense-of-children-behaving-badly.html

4. Learn more about Mawi at http://en.wikipedia.org/wiki/Selamawi_Asgedom

5. See www.ctcl.org

6. Loren Pope, *Colleges That Change Lives: 40 Schools That Will Change the Way You Think about Colleges* (New York: Penguin, 2006).

7. Sharon Biggs, "A child's brain fully develops by age 25," Examiner.com, September 21, 2009; http://www.examiner.com/parenting-education-in-newark/a-child-s-brain-fully-develops-by-age-25

8. Here's a good chart that gives milestones from birth through five years old. There are many more such charts online. http://www.cdc.gov/ncbddd/actearly/milestones/

9. "The brain doesn't hit adult levels until the age of twenty-five." (Jay Giedd, "The Adolescent Brain—Why Teenagers Think and Act Differently," *National Institute of Mental Health*; http://www.edinformatics.com/news/teenage_brains .htm)

Chapter 9: Eating Dinner

1. The National Center on Alcohol and Substance Abuse (CASA) at Columbia University, 2010.

2. *Archives of Pediatrics and Adolescent Medicine,* 2004.

3. D. Neumark-Sztainer, et al. (University of Minnesota) *Arch Pediatric Adolesc Med.* January 2008; 162(1): 17-22.

4. American Dietetic Association Family Nutrition and Physical Activity Survey 2010.

5. Grace Freedman, Eatdinner.org, "About"; http://www.eat dinner.org/p/about.html

6. Rachel Stone, from a personal e-mail to the author, October 28, 2011.

7. Rachel Stone, "A 'Proof' of True Christian Faith," *Eat with Joy*, October 15, 2011; http://eatwithjoy.org/2011/10/15/ a-"proof"-of-true-christian-faith

Chapter 10: Parenting after Orange Alert

1. Homeland Security, "National Terrorism Advisory System"; http://www.dhs.gov/files/programs/ntas.shtm

2. Dr. Phil McGraw, *Family First: Your Step-by-Step Plan for Creating a Phenomenal Family* (New York: Simon and Schuster, 2004), 182.

Chapter 12: Baleen Whales, Taco Night, and the Cheese Stick Bubbler

1. Melinda Beck, "Blanks for the Memories," *Wall Street Journal,* May 31, 2011; http://online.wsj.com/article/SB100014240527 02304520804576341482658082052.html

2. Salman Rushdie, *Haroun and the Sea of Stories* (London: Penguin, 1991), 63.

Acknowledgments

1. Bruce Cockburn, "Don't Feel Your Touch," June 1997; on the album *Big Circumstance*, 1988.

ABOUT THE AUTHOR

As a freelance writer, **Jennifer Grant** has written about everything from baby slings to bioterrorism to badly behaving celebrities. Her first book, *Love You More: The Divine Surprise of Adopting My Daughter*, was published in 2011. She currently writes about health and family for the *Chicago Tribune* and on popular culture and new books for *Christianity Today*'s her.meneutics blog. Grant is a proud founding member of Redbud Writers Guild. She lives with her husband, David, and their four children outside of Chicago, Illinois. Find her online at jennifergrant.com.

WORTHY

PUBLISHING

IF YOU LIKED THIS BOOK . . .

- Tell your friends by going to: www.momumental.org and clicking "LIKE"
- Share the video book trailer by posting it on your Facebook page
- Head over to facebook.com/MOMumentalBook, click "LIKE" and post a comment regarding what you enjoyed about the book
- Tweet "I recommend reading #MOMumentalBook by @jennifercgrant @Worthypub"
- Hashtag: #MOMumentalBook
- Subscribe to our newsletter by going to www.worthy publishing.com

WORTHY PUBLISHING
FACEBOOK PAGE

WORTHY PUBLISHING
WEBSITE